Rapid Assessment Process

Rapid Assessment Process

An Introduction

James Beebe

ALTAMIRA
PRESS

A Division of Rowman & Littlefield Publishers, Inc.
Walnut Creek • Lanham • New York • Oxford

ALTAMIRA
P R E S S

A Division of Rowman & Littlefield Publishers, Inc.
1630 North Main Street, #367
Walnut Creek, CA 94596
www.altamirapress.com

Rowman & Littlefield Publishers, Inc.
4720 Boston Way
Lanham, MD 20706

12 Hid's Copse Road
Cumnor Hill, Oxford OX2 9JJ, England

British Library Cataloguing in Publication Information Available

Library of Congress Cataloging-in-Publication Data

Beebe, James
   Rapid assessment process : an introduction / James Beebe.
   p. cm.
   ISBN 0-7591-0011-X (cloth : alk. paper) — ISBN 0-7591-0012-8 (pbk. : alk. paper)
   1. Evaluation research (Social sciences) 2. Social sciences—Methodology. I. Title.

H62 .B3537 201
300'.7'2—dc21

                                      2001022067

Printed in the United States of America

∞™ The paper used in this publication meets the minimum requirements of American
National Standard for Information Sciences—Permanence of Paper for Printed Library
Materials, ANSI/NISO Z39.48-1992.

CONTENTS

CONTENTS

CONTENTS

FIGURES

PREFACE

When I was a Peace Corps Volunteer in the Philippines I quickly learned that I needed to know the meanings people there attached to words, because I could not assume we assigned the same meanings to the same words. Even something as straightforward as offering a soft drink to someone was subject to misunderstanding and embarrassment, regardless of whether the offer was made in the local language or in English. The offer was made, the response was "Thank you," and my expectation was that the offer had been accepted. I delivered the soft drink to someone who did not want it and discovered that the "Thank you" was gratitude for the offer and not an acceptance of it. Graduate studies at the University of the Philippines and Stanford, including a year of fieldwork in a village in the Philippines, introduced me to the vocabulary and the methodology of anthropology and helped me begin to understand the requirements for successful crosscultural communication.

After graduate school, I joined the U.S. Agency for International Development (USAID) and spent the next eighteen years as a practitioner helping to implement foreign assistance projects. I spent more than fourteen of these years overseas, serving long-term assignments in Sudan, the Philippines, Liberia, and South Africa. These experiences reinforced for me the need to pay attention to the categories used by others and the meanings they attached to the words they used (see Emic and Etic, p. 33 in chapter 2). I soon realized that successful interventions have to be based on genuine partnership between outsiders who often control access to resources and the insiders who will ultimately be responsible for implementing changes. Partnership in designing interventions is critical for their success. The potential for miscommunication is always present when outsiders and insiders attempt to collaborate on the design of an intervention as well as on implementation, monitoring, and evaluation. To minimize miscommunication we need to recognize that categories and meaning are socially constructed. Meanings of words depend upon their cultural context. We ignore the context at our peril. Qualitative, ethnographic research can improve the communication process, but often neither the time nor other resources are available for traditional approaches to this type of research. The need for a qualitative approach that can be done quickly provides the rationale for Rapid Assessment Process (RAP). It is my position that RAP provides an extremely useful tool in many situations, but that there are minimum conditions that must be satisfied before the inquiry is labeled as RAP and that even when RAP is implemented carefully, its limitations must be recognized.

Acknowledgments

Several events and individuals have contributed significantly to my involvement with RAP and to the development of this book. In 1982, the USAID mission in the Sudan allowed me to experiment with Rapid Appraisal during a week-long visit to a village in the western Sudan. The second of the two examples of RAP at the beginning of chapter 1 is a brief description of this experience. I returned from this experience convinced of the value of even short-term qualitative fieldwork (Beebe 1982). I also returned with numerous questions concerning the process that had produced these results. During the next several years there were reports from sites all over the world where people were implementing Rapid Rural Appraisals.

In 1985 Khon Kaen University in northeast Thailand and the Ford Foundation sponsored my attendance at the International Conference on Rapid Rural Appraisal at Khon Kaen University (Khon Kaen University 1987). During a small group session at this conference, Terry Grandstaff, M.A. Hamid, Neil Jamieson, and I started the process of identifying and labeling the essential principles of Rapid Appraisal. The conceptual framework used in this book originated in these discussions.

While attending the conference, I met Robert Chambers and had the wonderful opportunity of being with him during a visit to a village close to Khon Kaen University. This visit/fieldwork was designed as a practice session to provide an introduction to Rapid Appraisal. Given the constraints of time and the lack of prior preparation, I was very impressed with Chambers's approach. He started the exchange with a farmer by quickly communicating his respect and defined the role of the farmer as the expert and the role of the visitors as students wanting to learn. The farmer responded by sharing with the team an amazing amount of information in a few minutes. Chambers listened carefully to what the farmer had to say, even while he was observing the environment and using what he saw to direct the conversation. He made a special effort to involve all the other team members in the process.

For more than twenty-five years, Chambers has been a leader in defining and popularizing rapid research techniques. His clear writing, devoid of the jargon of the social sciences, and his use of choice phrases that capture the essence of the approach have helped introduce rapid research methods to people worldwide. During the last decade, Chambers has advocated making the process participatory and shifting the focus away from rapid to "relaxed" (Chambers 1999). I owe Chambers a special thanks for his leadership in developing and popularizing rapid research methods.

Mitch Allen of AltaMira Press first suggested I write this book in 1991. It took me almost ten years of additional experience and a change of careers before I could actually write it. I appreciate Mitch Allen's patience and continued confidence.

By 1993 I had reformulated the basic concepts that define Rapid Appraisal and presented them in a paper at a workshop sponsored by the Washington Association of Professional Anthropologists and the applied anthropology program at the American University. In 1995 an expanded version of that paper was published in *Human Organization* (Beebe 1995).

In 1996 I joined the faculty of the Doctoral Program in Leadership Studies at Gonzaga University. Teaching qualitative research forced me to reconsider the relationship between Rapid Appraisal and ethnography as an approach to qualitative research. I started exploring the relationship between the intensive teamwork associated with Rapid Appraisal and the prolonged fieldwork associated with ethnography. My students have not been shy in pointing out the gaps in my work, and they have convinced me of the need to significantly expand the presentation. I owe a special debt to the students in my summer 1999, fall 1999, and summer 2000 qualitative methodology classes, who helped with drafts of the book: Dale Abendroth, Elaine Ackerman, Mary Alberts, Una Alderman, Carol Allen, Denise Arnold, Earl Bartmess, Thomas Camm, Nancy Chase, Debra Clemens, Albert Fein, Steve Finch, Craig Hinnenkamp, Rhonda Horobiowski, Kevin Hoyer, Lori Johnson, Janet Katz, Connie Kliewer, Grace Leaf, Kristine Lesperance, Cherisse Luxa, John Lyons, Robert McCann, Susan McIntyre, Matt Mitchell, Barbara Morrison, LaQuitta Moultrie, Michelle O'Neill, David Perry, Jonathan Reams, Marilyn Reilly, Robert Smart, Sandra Smith, Sharon Wessman, Kathryn Whalen, Nancy Bagley, and Terence Young.

A RAP involving several students from the fall 1999 class provides the other example at the beginning of chapter 1. This RAP was critical for identifying implementation issues, such as the role of the insider on the team, and is discussed in some detail in chapter 4.

I acknowledge the intellectual companionship of my colleagues and their contribution to my thinking about RAP. I especially appreciate the helpful comments on this and earlier versions of this work by Maria Beebe, Andrea Harper, Maria Hizon, Cherisse Luxa, Harold McArthur, Marion McNamara, June Miller, Georgeta Munteah, Perry Phillip, Marleen Ramsey, and Rochelle Rainey. Obviously, any omissions or errors are my responsibility. I look forward to receiving feedback on this book and encourage my readers to share their views, questions, and comments. These can be sent by e-mail to beebe@gonzaga.edu or by regular mail to James Beebe, Doctoral Program in Leadership Studies, Gonzaga University, 502 E. Boone Ave., Spokane, WA 99258.

INTRODUCTION

My experience has convinced me that, in a relatively short time, a multi-disciplinary research team, including **insiders** as well as outsiders, can make significant progress toward understanding a problematic situation. My objective in writing this book is to convince you that such an approach is possible, to provide you with enough examples and information about specific techniques that you will be willing to experiment with the approach, and to ensure that you recognize its limits. The approach is called **Rapid Assessment Process, or RAP,** and is defined as

> intensive, team-based qualitative inquiry using **triangulation,** iterative data analysis and additional **data collection** to quickly develop a preliminary understanding of a situation from the insider's perspective.

The phrase "intensive, team-based qualitative inquiry" makes explicit that the process is intensive. Miles and Huberman (1994, 6) note that research can be conducted through intense or prolonged **fieldwork**. Inquiry is implemented by a RAP team and not by individual researchers. I have chosen the phrase "qualitative inquiry" instead of "**ethnography**" out of respect for those who have helped define ethnography and argue it always requires prolonged fieldwork. The primary means for data collection is to talk with people and to get them to tell their stories, as opposed to answering your questions.

Why Rapid Assessment Process?

RAP is similar to Hildebrand's (1982) **"Sondeo"** method and what for the last twenty-five years has been called **"Rapid Appraisal,"** "Rapid Assessment," or **"Rapid Rural Appraisal."** Research approaches having at least some of the characteristics of RAP have also been referred to by a variety of names and have been used in numerous settings, in the United States and throughout the world. These are discussed in chapter 8.

I have chosen to use the phrase "Rapid Assessment Process" because I believe each of the words helps define the methodology and because the acronym "RAP" communicates the essential ingredient for successful implementation. The objective of RAP is not to elicit answers to questions, or even to talk with others, but to communicate with them using their vocabulary and rhythm. One definition of rap is "to talk freely and frankly." As discussed in chapter 9, the acronym "RAP" has been widely used by a variety of authors to describe this type of research.

As used in the phrase "Rapid Assessment Process," the word "Rapid" means a minimum of four days and, in most situations, a maximum of six weeks. RAP recognizes that there are times when results are needed almost immediately and that the "rapid" production of results involves compromises and requires special attention to methodology if the results are to be meaningful. Rapid does not mean rushed, and spending too little time or being rushed during the process can reduce RAP to "research tourism."

"Assessment" and "appraisal" are synonyms and both terms "Rapid Assessment" and "Rapid Appraisal" have been widely used. One definition of "assess" is "to determine the importance, size, or value," while "assessment" is defined as "the act or an instance of assessing" (Merriam-Webster 1993, 69). I have not used "appraisal" because that term has become so closely associated with development projects, especially projects funded by multilateral donors like the World Bank, that use of the term would lead to confusion and might limit the potential application of RAP.

"Process" as used in the phrase "Rapid Assessment Process" means "a series of actions or operations conducing to an end" (Merriam-Webster 1993, 929). A process approach suggests that at least as much attention is given to the way results are obtained as to the results themselves. I like "process." Different authors have used a variety of words ("program," "procedure," "practice," "protocol") to force the acronym to spell RAP with apparently very little difference in meaning.

Rationale for This Book

I believe RAP can produce useful results even when the most important elements of the local situations from the perspective of the local **participants** are not obvious. Often in these situations the words the local participants use to define the situation, their categories for dealing with reality, are also not known. If there is no urgent need for an intervention to address the situation, traditional, long-term fieldwork is a solution. However, my experience has been that there is almost never enough time, that when there is time, trained qualitative researchers are not available, and that when both are available, it is almost impossible to convince the decision makers that long-term **qualitative research** is the best use of resources.

The primary goal of this book is to encourage new users to experiment with RAP, but there are two additional goals: (1) helping current users of RAP do a better job and (2) instilling confidence in the results of RAP among the decision makers who are its potential clients. Students studying qualitative research methods, especially students in professional programs, are an important audience for this book. These students can be found in graduate and undergraduate courses as diverse as community nursing, advanced agricultural research, rural sociology, forestry, marine management, community development, leadership studies, organizational theory, qualitative research, information systems planning, and urban planning. Professionals facing complex situations where local categories are not known, but who do not have the time or resources for traditional long-term fieldwork, are a second audience. Rapid research approaches have been used for project design, project evaluation, and for design of additional research in fields as diverse as wetland evaluation, city-wide needs assessment, early childhood care, home ownership patterns among minorities, reproductive health, marketing, and landscape planning.

RAP uses many of the techniques of qualitative research. These techniques should be familiar to anyone with formal training in anthropology or closely related fields. Ideally, every RAP team will have at least one member with expertise in the assumptions and techniques of qualitative research. However, there will be times when no one on the team has had formal training in qualitative research methodology, or when most team members will be unfamiliar with these techniques. Therefore, I have included brief introductions to some concepts most useful to RAP and suggestions on where additional information can be found. A note of caution—these brief introductions cannot do justice to the richness of qualitative research and the reader may wish to seek further information from primary sources. However, even these brief introductions, when combined with a student's attitude, a willingness to listen intently, and genuine respect for others can help practitioners get started. The specific techniques that are introduced have proven to be especially relevant to RAP. If no one on the team has experience with qualitative research methodology, this should be noted in the report.

My decision to produce a book that can be used in both academic and nonacademic settings will probably ensure that neither camp is completely satisfied with the results.

Organization

I have organized the book around the two basic concepts of RAP: (1) data collection using triangulation and (2) analysis using an **iterative process** where initial analysis is followed by several cycles of additional data collection and more analysis. Chapter 1 discusses two examples of RAP, explores situations where RAP may be especially appropriate, and provides an overview of the relationship of specific research techniques to the basic concepts of RAP. Figure 1.1 on page 9 of chapter 1 is a navigational aide and includes page numbers for quickly locating information about both basic concepts and techniques. Chapter 2 deals with data collection and is divided between (1) an introduction to the concept of triangulation along with discussion of illustrative techniques associated with triangulation and (2) an introduction to concepts relevant to collecting data in a way that gets at the insider's perspective. Chapter 3 deals with iterative analysis and additional data collection and is divided between (1) an introduction to the iterative process along with a discussion of illustrative techniques associated with the iterative process and (2) a discussion of data analysis and illustrative techniques for data analysis. The materials in the first parts of chapters 2 and 3 are especially critical for the teamwork that is the foundation of RAP. The materials in the latter parts of chapters 2 and 3 provide an introduction to research techniques that will already be familiar to anyone with training in qualitative research. Chapter 4 explores the special role of teamwork in RAP and is based on RAPs of the Student Services Division at a community college and state farms in Poland. Chapter 5 examines issues relating to the trustworthiness of RAP's results, notes concerns about the process, and proposes the use of a checklist, the "RAP sheet," to be attached to RAP reports. The checklist is designed to provide enough information about the research that a reader can evaluate the results, and to remind the RAP team of issues they should not overlook. Chapter 6 focuses on specific suggestions for making RAP more successful. Chapter 7 examines the relationship of the RAP team to the sponsoring organization and discusses the issue of **bogus empowerment**. Chapter 8 provides the context for relating RAP to other rapid methods by briefly reviewing the history of RAP, the rationale behind the term RAP, and the issues of **Appreciative Inquiry** and participatory research. Chapter 8 also includes a list of other **rapid research methods** that is organized around the sectors where these methods have been used. Finally, the appendix includes suggestions for learning about RAP by doing a condensed form of RAP called a "Mini-RAP."

Terms in bold are defined in the glossary. Where appropriate, chapters include the identification of main points and suggestions for additional readings. Items from the "Essential RAPper Library" below are repeated in the appropriate "Additional Readings" sections of individual chapters.

Additional Readings: The Essential RAPper Library

In preparing the following list of essential books, I have started with the assumption that expertise in qualitative research methodology is valuable for the RAP team. I have also assumed that there will be times when no one on the team has had prior training in qualitative research methodology and that books can provide access to some of the needed expertise. Students in qualitative research courses will find that other books used in their courses also cover the topics in these books. The following books provide both an introduction to the philosophy that underlies qualitative research,

and to the attitudes necessary to implement it, and details on specific research techniques, including data analysis and preparation of results, relevant to the successful completion of a qualitative research project.

Bernard, H. R. 1995. *Research methods in anthropology: Qualitative and quantitative approaches.* 2d ed. Walnut Creek, Calif.: AltaMira.

Creswell, J. W. 1998. *Qualitative inquiry and research design: Choosing among
five traditions.* Thousand Oaks, Calif.: Sage.

Ely, M., M. Anzul, T. Friedman, D. Garner, and A. M. Steinmetz 1991. *Doing qualitative research: Circles within circles.* Bristol, Pa.: Falmer Press.

Marshall, C., and G. B. Rossman. 1999. *Designing qualitative research.* 3d ed.
Thousand Oaks, Calif.: Sage.

Miles, M. B., and M. A. Huberman. 1994. *Qualitative data analysis: An expanded sourcebook.* 2d ed. Thousand Oaks, Calif.: Sage.

The American Anthropological Association's *Anthropology Resources
on the Internet,* at <http://www.ameranthassn.org/resinet.htm>, lists numerous sites with links to anthropology resources. There is an enormous
amount of free material now available on the Internet.

TO RAP OR NOT TO RAP (AND THE BASIC CONCEPTS)

Main Points

1. RAP is intensive, team-based ethnographic inquiry using triangulation, iterative data analysis, and additional data collection to quickly develop a preliminary understanding of a situation from the insider's perspective.

2. The phrase "Rapid Assessment Process" defines the methodology and the acronym, RAP, communicates the essential ingredient for successful implementation.

3. RAP allows a team of at least two individuals to quickly gain sufficient understanding of a situation to make preliminary decisions for the design and implementation of applied activities or additional research.

4. Results can be produced in as few as four days, but implementation more typically requires several weeks.

5. RAP uses the techniques and shares many of the characteristics of ethnography, but differs in two important ways: (1) more than one researcher is always involved in data collection and teamwork is essential for data triangulation; (2) more than one researcher is involved in an iterative approach to data analysis and additional data collection.

6. The intensive teamwork for data collection and analysis is an alternative to prolonged fieldwork and produces results that provide insights into the perspective and worldly view of the participants in the local system.

7. RAP is especially appropriate for a variety of situations where qualitative research is needed.

8. RAP can be used for monitoring and evaluation.

9. Sometimes survey research is not an option for initial research because not enough is known to prepare the questionnaire.

Example One: Student Services at a Community College

The new dean at a community college in the Pacific Northwest was made to understand during her interview for the position that there was serious discord in the Student Services Division. After being offered the position, Pat (a pseudonym) was told that she was expected to contribute to a "healing" process. By November of Pat's first term, she realized the rift was greater than she had anticipated, but that many of her actions to bring about change were being warmly received by many in the division. Pat knew that there were no easy solutions to the organizational **culture** issues in the division, and hoped that an examination of this culture could contribute to reconciliation and help individuals refocus on the mission of the division and the college. Pat instinctively knew that the history of the different conflicts was too long and the issues too complex for research based on a set of questions to be administered to everyone. She assumed that there would be a very low level of participation in research based on questionnaires, even if appropriate questions could be identified. Pat also knew that the community college did not have the luxury of the extensive time and other resources required for traditional qualitative research. At this point, she requested a Rapid Assessment Process of the organizational culture of the division. She knew that the goal of RAP was to *listen* to the stories of individuals involved in an organization and from these stories to quickly identify common themes.

Most of the participants' comments were grouped into categories and identified as constraints to the ability of the people involved in the Student Services Division to do the best job possible. There was a general consensus that performance was not always as good as it should be, and that most people truly wanted to do better, but that there were a range of interrelated factors that prevented this from happening. The six constraints identified involved: (1) communication; (2) physical space; (3) technology; (4) utilization of people's time, talents, and creativity; (5) increases in the number and complexity of regulations; and (6) inadequate resources.

While there was general agreement that the purpose of working in student services was to provide services to students, there was significant disagreement about the characteristics of the student population and what it meant to serve them. "Students are the reason why I'm here" was a view expressed by almost everyone interviewed. Several individuals, however, objected to the use of the word "service" to describe the relationship with students. One participant suggested that students view services as things they are entitled to and people who provide services as their servants. For some participants, the defining characteristic of service was being "available." This was identified as being an especially important aspect of service for "walk-in traffic." Most participants appeared to recognize a difference between students needing merely "regular" services, such as academic advising, and "high-maintenance" students needing help with issues such as immigration/visa problems and emotional and mental-health problems.

Several participants consistently used the words "customers" or "clients" instead of "students." There was significant disagreement about the characteristics of the student population and how this had changed over time. Some indicated that "our students have always had special needs," while others pointed to a growing trend in "emergent situational disorders that happen as a result of overstress in personal academic life choices." A few participants noted their students were less prepared for college now than students in the past had been; one participant said, "students do not comprehend written communication and have trouble with verbal communication." Another participant noted, "We are doing more handholding than we used to do." One person, who had worked at the college for over three decades, said there had been a change in general life experiences that affected preparedness, especially with regard to readiness in a professional/technical arena. Another participant shared a story told to him by one of the technical instructors of a student who was asked to get a Phillips screwdriver from the tool crib, and who returned empty-handed, saying that all he could find was a "Stanley."

Several participants expressed surprise that changes in the characteristics of the student population were even being discussed. "I wasn't aware that there are major changes" in the student population, one participant commented. One participant suggested that perhaps the changes were not in the students, but in the staff, saying that the staff had grown older and that maturity had changed perceptions. "I'm not the bleeding heart liberal I was when I started," this participant added. Some students were described as aggressive and "bullish" in demanding services from staff, "expecting everything to be given to them and believing it's always someone else's fault when things went wrong." Other students were described as lacking sufficient skills to request services they needed and were entitled to. The argument was that, for some students, services should include advocacy on behalf of the students. An individual dealing with special population students offered a plea for greater effort be made to ensure that "no one drops between the cracks" and that his colleagues should realize that this request was not for special advantages, but for a "level playing field."

Teams were organized around the constraints identified by the RAP and everyone working in the division was asked to participate on at least one team. Funding was identified that teams could apply for to address some of the constraints. The identification of serious differences in how individuals who work in the division understand the terms "students" and "services" has made possible constructive dialogue between the different factions.

Example Two: Village in the Western Sudan

The soils are sandy, the rain sparse and unpredictable, and the temperatures often above 110°F at the edge of the Sahara Desert in the western Sudan. Here, rural families survive during the better years through a combination of agriculture, livestock, and submission to the will of Allah. Margins for error are extremely slim. The adoption of an inappropriate agricultural intervention could mean ruin for the family and irreversible damage to the environment.

In the early 1980s the U.S. Agency for International Development was providing assistance to Sudan to establish an agricultural research center in western Sudan to help address these issues. The survival strategies of rural households in that environment were not understood. Mohamed el Obeid, a Sudanese agricultural development specialist, and I spent one week in 1982 in a village northwest of al Ubayyid (el Obeid), the provisional capital of North Kordofan (Beebe 1982). My objective was to experiment with the new research methodology called "Rapid Appraisal." The time in the village was amazing. We spent our days talking with groups of farmers or individuals. We conducted interviews about farming practices in the farmers' fields. We had extensive conversations with the village religious leader and the owner of the only shop (one of only two structures made of sun-dried bricks in a village where all the other structures were made of grain stalks and straw). We visited a slightly larger village where farmers could sell grain and other agricultural products. We spent our nights trying to figure out what we had learned and were often joined by men from the village who used our presence as an opportunity to discuss life in general, including the plans of one of the slightly more prosperous inhabitants to take a second wife. The structure imposed by the Rapid Appraisal methodology allowed us to quickly understand some of the important concerns of the residents of the area. Prior to our visit to this village, the assumption of both Sudanese and American agricultural research scientists had been that individual farmers were free to move at any time between gum arabic production (using the nitrogen-fixing tree *Acacia senegal*) and field crops such as sorghum and millet. Attention to their descriptions of crop rotations, especially when this was discussed with farmers in their fields, where crops could be observed, suggested that decisions by a farmer's neighbors could be a significant constraint. If a neighbor's large gum arabic trees, which would harbor birds, were too near, this would prevent the farmer from planting field crops until the neighbor was also ready to cut down his gum arabic trees and plant field crops. Subsequent research by Reeves and Frankenberger (1981) on agricultural practices in North Kordofan showed that adjacent fields were often cultivated by farmers who were related and that this also played a role in timing the rotation of a field from gum arabic production to field crops. Recognition of constraints on the decision-making abilities of individual farmers had a significant impact on the approach to farming systems research and extension proposed for the western Sudan.

The Need for the Insider's Perspective

Despite the many kilometers that separate the village in western Sudan and the community college in eastern Washington, the two situations share an important characteristic. Both are complicated situations where initially not enough was known to develop a questionnaire. Only the insiders in each of these situations were in a position to define the elements of their systems and identify those elements that were most relevant to the issues they faced. The insiders in the Sudanese village knew at least intuitively that they could not change their crop-rotation pattern without regard to the actions of their neighbors, but it is unlikely that a question could have been formulated in advance that would have elicited this information. Likewise, it is unlikely that a question could have been developed to elicit information on the different ways staff at the community college defined students and services, since there was no reason for outsiders (or even many of the insiders) to think this was an issue. Another characteristic shared by these two situations was that results were needed quickly and that, even if the results had not been needed quickly, there were not sufficient resources for traditional, long-term fieldwork. The approach to research that focuses on getting the insider's perspective is referred to as "qualitative" research or inquiry. It is useful under some circumstances to differentiate between qualitative research and an approach to qualitative research called "ethnographic" research. They are, however, often used interchangeably. In chapter 2, I will return to the relationship between the insider's perspective and ethnographic/qualitative research (see Ethnography, p. 30; Emic and Etic, p. 33).

Rapid Assessment Process and Intensive Team Interaction

RAPs similar to what was done at the community college in the Pacific Northwest and in the village in western Sudan provide a way to investigate complicated situations in which issues are not yet well defined and where there is not sufficient time (or other resources) for long-term ethnographic research. RAP shares many of the characteristics of ethnographic research. RAP, however, substitutes intensive, team interaction in both the collection and analysis of data for the prolonged fieldwork normally associated with ethnography. RAP will produce solid qualitative results that can be expected to be different from those produced by longer-term fieldwork. In some cases, intensive team interaction over a short period may produce better results than a lone researcher over a long period. RAP will almost always produce results in a fraction of the time and at less cost than traditional ethnography.

Basic Concepts

RAP uses the techniques and shares many of the characteristics of ethnography, but differs in two important ways: (1) more than one researcher is always involved in data collection and the teamwork is essential for data triangulation; (2) more than one researcher is involved in an iterative approach to data analysis and additional data collection. The intensive teamwork for both the data collection and analysis is an alternative to prolonged fieldwork and produces qualitative results. RAP allows a team of at least two individuals to quickly gain sufficient understanding of a situation to make preliminary decisions for the design and implementation of applied activities or additional research. Results can be produced in one to six weeks. While the time period for RAP is recognized as arbitrary, my experience has convinced me that a minimum of four days is required for iterative data analysis and additional data collection, an issue I will return to in subsequent chapters (see Too Little or Too Much Time, p. 105).

The two basic concepts of RAP define its relationship with traditional ethnography and allow results to be produced quickly. The two basic concepts are

1. intensive teamwork as part of the triangulation of data collection, and

2. intensive teamwork during the iterative process of data analysis and additional data collection.

Adherence to these concepts can provide a flexible but rigorous approach to the rapid collection and analysis of data.

Relationship of the Basic Concepts to Research Techniques

RAP is defined by the basic concepts of triangulation and iterative analysis, and additional data collection, and NOT by the use of specific research techniques.

RAP is defined by its two basic concepts instead of by a specific set of research techniques. While, traditionally, some research techniques have been associated with rapid research methods, these methods are not necessarily required. Specific research techniques for use in a given RAP are

7

chosen from among a wide range of techniques available to qualitative researchers and are chosen based on the specific topic being investigated and the resources available to the team. Specific techniques used in a RAP can vary significantly depending on the situation.

Figure 1.1 illustrates the relationship of the basic concepts and illustrative research techniques associated with them. As noted above, the listed research techniques are not the only way of achieving the basic concepts, but are techniques that have been found to work together under some field conditions.

Conditions Where RAP Is Especially Appropriate

I have identified, as the type of situation where RAP may be the most appropriate methodology, complex situations where the categories and words used by the local people involved in a situation are not known. I will try to make the case throughout this book that if results are needed immediately, RAP may be the only choice. RAP is also appropriate for a variety of situations where qualitative research is needed, even if there is no time constraint. Creswell (1998, 17–18) has identified what he calls compelling reasons for undertaking a qualitative study as opposed to a quantitative study. These reasons can help identify situations where RAP is an appropriate approach for research:

1. When a topic needs to be explored. This occurs when there is insufficient information available to identify variables or to know how local people identify them.

2. When the question begins with "how" or "what." These are the questions when the critical elements in a situation and their relationship to each other cannot be identified.

3. When there is a need for a detailed view. Situations may be so site specific that general information, especially information that covers a larger area or very many people, may not provide insight into the issue being investigated. There are times when only detailed information on a limited topic is useful.

CONCEPT 1. TRIANGULATION and DATA COLLECTION

Triangulation	*Illustrative Techniques for Triangulation*
Triangulation, 18	Team Membership, 24
Triangulation and the	Team Interviewing, 26
Insider's Perspective, 18	Team Observing, 27
Triangulation and RAP, 22	Team Collection of Information, 27
Data Collection	*Illustrative Techniques for Data Collection*
Data Collection to Get the	Semistructured Interviews, 35
Insider's Perspective, 28	Use of Short Guidelines, 40
—Qualitative Research, 29	Use of a Tape Recorder, 41
—Ethnography, 30	Use of Interpreters, 43
—Culture, 32	Selection of Respondents, 45
—Emic and Etic, 33	Individuals and Focus Groups, 46
—Indigenous Knowledge, 34	Structured Interviews, 47
—Variability, 35	Comparing and Sorting Objects, 48
	Participant Observation, 48
	Unobtrusive Observations, 49
	Folk Tales and Other Verbal Lore, 50
	Systems, Soft Systems, and Rich Pictures, 50
	Mapping, 52
	Field Notes and Logs, 54

CONCEPT 2. ITERATIVE ANALYSIS AND ADDITIONAL DATA COLLECTION

The Iterative Process	*Illustrative Techniques Associated with the Iterative Process*
Iteration, 60	Structuring the Research Time, 62
Iteration and Ethnography, 60	Checking Back with Informants, 63
Iteration and RAP, 61	RAP Report Preparation, 64
Data Analysis	*Illustrative Techniques for Data Analysis*
Data Analysis, 65	Coding, 66
	Data Display, 68
	Conclusion Drawing and Verification, 69
	How Much Data Is Needed?, 73
	Checking Back with Informants, 73

Figure 1.1 Relationship of the Basic Concepts and Illustrative Techniques

4. When there is a need to study individuals in their natural setting. Without access to the environment of the person providing answers, it may not be possible to know what questions should be asked or to understand the context for the answers

given. If participants are removed from their setting, it may lead to contrived findings that are out of context.

5. When there is a need to emphasize the researcher's role as a partner instead of as an expert. There is growing recognition that research needs to be collaborative with all parties that stand to benefit. People have limited tolerance for experts who pass judgment on them. People increasingly are demanding that they be allowed to articulate their own stories.

RAP is not an appropriate methodology if quantifiable results are needed, such as the percent of individuals, opinions, and homes in different categories. RAP may be the appropriate methodology for identifying the most relevant categories, and the most appropriate labels for these categories, but the research to collect and analyze such data is usually not a part of RAP.

RAP may not be appropriate if numbers or percents are needed.

Using RAP for Monitoring, Evaluation, and Midcourse Corrections

RAP can be used for monitoring and evaluation. The identification of specific midcourse corrections during the implementation of an activity is another task for which a RAP may be useful. When ongoing monitoring of an activity suggests problems with implementation and the causes of these problems are not obvious, a RAP team can explore questions as fundamental as whether the local people and the parties responsible for the activity agree on what constitutes success and failure. A RAP approach is especially useful in identifying the unexpected. A report based on a few weeks work and delivered immediately allows for midcourse corrections. A report prepared by a team in a situation where local people have been full partners increases the chances that recommendations for changes can be implemented, and increases the opportunities to implement changes, even before the recommendations have been made formally.

When faced with the limitations of time and resources, the temptation can be to make a very quick visit with the most easily reached local participants. This is sometimes referred to as "**research tourism**." Another temptation is to do a questionnaire survey even when there is agreement that the most important issues have not yet been identified, and that the categories and words with the greatest relevance to the local people are not known. The rationale seems to be that something needs to be done, and that anything is better than either research tourism or nothing.

When Survey Research Is Not the Best Option

The story of the two neighboring villages in Africa, one where almost all the babies under one year of age were boys and another where almost all were girls, has become part of the folklore of health-care development workers. The villages were identified as a result of a survey of health and mothers' knowledge of health-care practices for children under one. The storyteller usually relates, empathetically, that the study was funded by a major international donor and implemented by a professional researcher who had carefully prepared the questionnaire and trained and supervised the field staff who carried out the interviews. The results were so surprising that local ministry personnel were sent to the villages to investigate. What they reported after their visits to these villages is more interesting than the original "results." The mothers in the first village considered boy babies much more desirable than girl babies and, when asked about their children, tended not to mention the girls. Thus the village appeared to have almost no girls. The mothers in the second village also considered boy babies more desirable than girl babies. However, in this village mothers did not tell strangers about their boys out of fear that if they brought attention to their sons, harm would seek out the boys. Thus the village appeared to have almost no boys. Like so much folklore, it is not possible to identify the source of this story.

Survey research based on questionnaires, a group of written questions to which individuals respond, have been used and misused worldwide. When faced with the need for information about situations, researchers have often tended to do a survey. Survey research has been viewed as reliable, producing similar answers every time the questionnaire is administered, and relatively quick when compared to traditional ethnographic research. My argument is that often survey research is not an option for initial research because not enough is known to prepare the questionnaire.

To prepare a questionnaire, you need to be able to identify the relevant elements of a situation, the specific categories that are important to the respondents, and the words they use for these categories. Since a questionnaire cannot identify unanticipated, site-specific relationships, it is limited to validating relationships articulated in advance.

Unless **questionnaire survey research** is based on the categories and vocabulary of the respondents and the context of the data is understood, the results may not be valid measures of what they purport to measure. Such results can be reliable without being valid, since different researchers administering similar questionnaires would likely get the same results.

An experiment by Stone and Campbell designed to examine the accuracy of practices, attitudes, and knowledge (PAK) surveys concerning fertility and family planning in Nepal illustrates this. Stone and Campbell hired and trained interviewers to administer the Nepal Fertility Survey to women in three villages. They then cross-checked the information on the survey forms by using other methods, including casual conversations and unstructured interviews. During the survey, 36 percent of the respondents claimed they had not heard of abortion. When Stone and Campbell asked about awareness of abortion, 100 percent knew about abortions and even "maintained that is was inconceivable that someone had not heard of [it]." Stone and Campbell suggest that part of the explanation is that abortion is considered a "religious sin" and that some respondents were "insulted by the question" (1984, 31). When they talked to the respondents who had indicated during the survey that they had not heard of abortion, every respondent had reinterpreted the question to make it more threatening. They found that respondents had interpreted the question on whether they had "heard of abortion" as a question on knowledge of technique or knowledge of who had had an abortion. They found that every woman who had reported little knowledge of family planning in the survey reported that they had difficulty understanding the questions and had been embarrassed by them.

> Some of them stressed that they were not able to respond to these questions because the interviewers were male. Others said it didn't matter so much that they were male, the problem was that they were strangers. And several women mentioned that they simply could not respond to the questions because other relatives and neighbors were present. (31)

Stone and Campbell identify cultural reinterpretation and problems of context as the factors that influenced the results and note that these can be problems for research done in the United States as well as research done overseas.

Specific problems have been identified with survey research on sexual behavior, voting, and geographical knowledge that may be relevant to other survey research as well. Clement suggests that there are two sources of error, invalid answers and volunteer bias, for research about sexual behavior. He notes that the validity of answers depends upon the ability of respondents to remember and their readiness to share the information, and that these are influenced by how the questions are posed (Clement 1990, 46). He specifically notes problems with crosscultural research, including research within the United States but at different universities or with different ethnic groups. Despite increases in the sophistication of survey research methodology and analysis for political/voting surveys, results have become less accurate. More and more individuals are simply refusing to provide answers to pollsters and increasing numbers identify themselves as "undecided," even when they have decided. Surveys on respondents' knowledge of geography have found "astonishing geographic ignorance." Phillips (1993) argues that these findings are the result of asking the wrong question. He notes that the questions are usually based on the categories used by geographers and not the mental images of people whose images are not "map-like." Phillips argues for the increased sensitivity to the nature of geographic mental representation as a basis to evaluate geographic knowledge. In all three of these examples, questions that fail to consider the cultural context with specific attention to the definitions and categories of the respondents have produced answers with limited validity.

It is sometimes incorrectly argued that survey research is quicker and can be done with less-experienced, less-qualified researchers, compared with RAP. Data collection by survey sometimes requires less time, but data analysis almost always takes more time. Data usually must be coded, entered into a computer, and then analyzed in separate steps and at places removed from the research site. Survey enumerators may have to make fewer independent decisions than a qualitative researcher does, but good survey research cannot be carried out without training and close field supervision. In addition, special training in instrument design and data management ensures that survey research usually does not include local participants as full members on the research team (Chambers 1991, 526).

> Beginning research on complex situations with questionnaires may result in the failure to identify important relationships.

RAP may identify the need for questionnaire survey research to supplement its results. As noted above, RAP cannot provide information on the percentages of respondents in different categories, and this information can be critical. Survey research can provide this type of information. However, RAP can provide the categories, vocabulary, and context necessary for the preparation of the questionnaire. The argument here is not against using questionnaire surveys, but against using them as the first step for trying to understand complex situations before local categories are known. In addition, a RAP may be a better starting point for some research because of its ability to discover relationships within the situation that may not have been anticipated. The use of techniques associated with RAP does not guarantee success in identifying important relationships, but initial research on complex situations based on a questionnaire often ensures that they will be missed.

The Need for Caution about the Use of RAP

Robert Chambers's observation concerning Rapid Appraisal also applies to RAP, in that there is a danger it "could be over-sold, too rapidly adopted, badly done, and then discredited, to suffer an undeserved, premature burial as has occurred with other innovative research approaches" (1991, 531). When numerical data is needed, RAP by itself will probably be an inappropriate methodology, but it might contribute to the design of a survey questionnaire to collect numerical data. When situations are especially complex or when an entire cycle, such as a growing season or a school year, needs to be investigated, long-term qualitative research may be necessary. There may be situations where it is culturally inappropriate for a team of researchers to interview an individual. Other valid reasons for concern about RAP include spending too little time on the activity, failure to consider the political and economic context, problems with team composition, choice of respondents and informants, and a failure to recognize a difference in power between the team and the local community. To date there has been a general lack of confirmation of RAP findings. RAP, along with other qualitative research methods, lacks credibility with some funding agencies, while other funding agencies have very unrealistic expectations about what RAP can accomplish and sometimes pressure researchers to do RAPs in inappropriate situations. These issues will be discussed in more detail in chapter 5 (see Problems with Credibility, p. 108).

There are numerous situations where RAP is inappropriate!

In the next chapter I will discuss the first of the two basic concepts, the one relating to data collection, triangulation, and intensive teamwork. Because of the importance of ethnography/qualitative research to RAP, I will spend time exploring it. However, since this is not intended to be a book about ethnography and qualitative research, issues can only be introduced and you are encouraged to refer to the additional readings listed at the end of the chapter for more information. The specific techniques that are introduced are those that have proven to be most relevant to RAP. Most of the techniques are designed to help facilitate the telling of stories as opposed to the eliciting of answers. Others are designed to ensure that the RAP team records data in ways that will make the data useful and easier to analyze. A specific RAP may use only a few of these techniques and may use other techniques that are not covered. One of the strengths of RAP is that it is not based on the use of a specific list of techniques.

Additional Readings

The readings listed below are some of the most-often cited references dealing with rapid research methods. Even though Scrimshaw and Gleason (1992) focuses on health programs, material in this book will be useful to researchers from a variety of fields. The full text of the Scrimshaw and Gleason book (as well as several other publications on rapid research methods) is available on-line at <http://www.unu.edu/unupress/food/foodnutrition,html>.

Chambers, R. 1991. Shortcut and participatory methods for gaining social information for projects. In *Putting people first: Sociological variables in rural development,* ed. M. M. Cernea, 515–37. 2d ed., Washington, D.C.: Oxford University Press, World Bank.

Khon Kaen University. 1987. *Proceedings of the 1985 International Conference on Rapid Rural Appraisal.* Khon Kaen, Thailand: Rural Systems Research and Farming Systems Research Projects.

Kumar, K. 1993. *Rapid appraisal methods.* Washington, D.C.: World Bank.

Scrimshaw, N., and G. R. Gleason. 1992. *Rapid assessment procedures: Qualitative methodologies for planning and evaluation of health related programmes.* Boston: International Nutrition Foundation for Developing Countries.

Van Willigen, J., and T. L. Finan. 1991. *Soundings: Rapid and reliable research methods for practicing anthropologists.* Washington, D.C.: American Anthropological Association.

DATA COLLECTION: TRIANGULATION AND GETTING THE INSIDER'S PERSPECTIVE

Main Points

1. The synergy resulting from triangulation based on intensive teamwork is absolutely crucial for RAP.

2. Intensive team interaction among RAP team members is an element of triangulation (along with team interaction for the iterative analysis and additional collection of data) and permits the RAP team to reduce significantly their time in the field.

3. The strength of RAP results from interaction among the RAP team members and the ability of the team to carry out triangulation at a very rapid rate.

4. By definition, RAP cannot be done by one person. Teams should be composed of a mix of insiders from and outsiders to the situation being investigated.

5. Intensive team interviewing is not based on sequential interviewing by members of the team, but on joint interviewing.

6. RAP and ethnography share many characteristics and specific research techniques.

7. **Semistructured interviews** based on guidelines are the key to RAP. The most important way of learning about local conditions is to ask local people.

8. The goal is to get people to talk on a subject and not just answer questions.

9. More than twenty techniques associated with ethnography and RAP are introduced in this chapter. To begin experimenting with RAP, all you need to remember is that your goal is to talk with people and to get them to tell their stories, as opposed to answering your questions.

Triangulation

An Example

The individual researcher sits across the desk from the director of the not-for-profit organization and asks her for details about the recent personnel crisis that appears to threaten the organization. The researcher is conscientious about trying to combine information he has collected in advance about the personnel issue with information he can collect by looking around as he conducts the interview, but problems making the tape recorder work distract him. About the only information he takes from this situation is what the director chooses to share with him during the interview.

Imagine this same scene, but with a team of researchers. This time a human relations/personnel specialist and a financial specialist join the lead researcher. One of the team members who will not be starting the interview takes care of the tape recorder. The lead researcher notices two fairly large stacks of unopened mail on a side table and opens the discussion with a reference to them. The comments by the director about her inability to keep up with events reminds the financial expert of the failure of the organization to complete a scheduled audit and he now joins the discussion. It becomes obvious that the personnel issues are not isolated. When the conversation turns to personnel, the human relations expert uses her expertise to ask about the rationale for some recent policy changes. She is sensitive to the feelings of the director and takes time to ensure that there is no appearance that this is "**tag-team interviewing**." The lead researcher notices that the human relations expert has not followed up on a potentially important comment by the director, and seeks clarification. By now you should get the picture. The same amount of time is spent on the interview, but the results are far richer than what the single researcher could have achieved. The results are even richer than what the three researchers could have achieved if each had separately interviewed the director.

Triangulation and the Insider's Perspective

Before exploring the relationship between RAP and triangulation based on intensive teamwork, it will be useful to briefly introduce the concept of triangulation. Because of the importance of triangulation to RAP and qualitative research in general, I will return to this topic in the section below on strategies for getting at the insider's perspective.

The term triangulation comes from navigation and physical survey-ing and describes an operation for finding a position or location by means of bearings from two known fixed points. For someone wanting to locate their position on a map, a single landmark can only provide the information that they are situated somewhere along a line in a par-ticular direction from that landmark. With two landmarks, however, their position can be pinpointed by taking bearings on both. They are at the point on the map where the two lines cross. Sometimes the ex-act location of these landmarks is not known, and triangulation can only identify a position in relation to the known points and not an ex-act point.

Triangulation has been used as a metaphor by social scientists for the use of data from different sources, the use of several different re-searchers, the use of multiple perspectives to interpret a single set of data, and the use of multiple methods to study a single problem. Even though the origin of triangulation refers to the use of three points, the term should not be taken literally; it is not limited to processes involv-ing three sources of data, researchers, perspectives, or methods (Janesick 1994, 215). The specific research techniques associated with triangulation are discussed later in this chapter. Intensive teamwork can increase the power of triangulation exponentially. Special requirements for successful teamwork, including a consideration of roles and leader-ship, are discussed in chapter 4.

Some social scientists have used the term "triangulation" to describe a strategy for establishing validity. Triangulation is seen as the combi-nation of methodologies for the study of a particular phenomenon (Flick 1992, 176) and it is used to test one source against another. Tri-angulation defined this way has been identified as "basic in ethno-graphic research" and at the heart of ethnographic validity (Fetterman 1989, 89). The assumption is that the researcher is searching for the convergence of at least two pieces of data (Ely et al. 1991, 97). It is fur-ther assumed that triangulation will result in a single valid proposition and thus validity will be confirmed.

When triangulation is focused exclusively on the convergence of ev-idence, Ely et al. (1991, 98) suggest, the other outcomes, inconsistency and contradiction, may be missed, although these are of greater value. Ely et al. suggest that the data that is inconsistent or contradictory are sometimes called negative cases. Negative case analysis is the search for evidence that does not fit into the emergent findings and that can lead to a reexamination of the findings (98).

Mathison is among the social scientists who suggest that convergence should not be expected. She notes that social phenomena are always complex and that triangulation should not be expected to provide a "clear path to a singular view of what is the case" (Mathison 1988, 15). For an increasing number of social scientists, triangulation is not a tool for validation, but an alternative to validation (Denzin and Lincoln 1994, 2). Since, according to Denzin, objective reality will never be captured, the goal of triangulation is the creation of fully grounded interpretive research (cited in Flick 1992, 180). For these social scientists, triangulation offers different perspectives and gives access to different versions of the phenomenon that is studied. Research is not intended to identify one reality against which results can be verified or falsified, but deals with different versions of the world (Flick 1992). Denzin and Lincoln argue that "the combination of multiple methods, empirical materials, perspectives, and observers in a single study is best understood then, as a strategy that adds rigor, breadth, and depth to any investigation" (1994, 2). Similar views are expressed by Flick (1992) and Fielding and Fielding (1986). Flick refers to the ability of triangulation to add "breadth and depth" without "artificial objectivation of the subject under study" (194). Fielding and Fielding suggest triangulation based on the addition of carefully and purposefully chosen methods is done to add "breadth or depth to our analysis, not for the purpose of pursuing 'objective' truth" (cited in Flick 1992, 179).

Four basic types of triangulation have been identified by Denzin and Lincoln (1994):

1. data triangulation is the use of a variety of data sources in a study;

2. investigator triangulation is the use of several different researchers or evaluators;

3. theory triangulation is the use of multiple perspectives to interpret a single set of data; and

4. methodological triangulation is the use of multiple methods to study a single problem.

Janesick (1994, 214–215) suggests a fifth basic type: interdisciplinary triangulation. She refers to the problem of the dominance of the discourse by a single discipline and uses the example of psychology in education. She claims that, because of psychology's dominance, there is a danger of aggregating individuals into sets of numbers and that this has moved us away from our understanding of lived experience. She advocates incorporating other disciplines, such as art, sociology, history, dance, and architecture, in the discourse.

Hammersley and Atkinson (1995, 230) expand the concept of data triangulation to include the comparison of data relating to the same phenomenon but deriving from different phases of the fieldwork and different points in the temporal cycles. They note that data triangulation can be based on the accounts of different participants, including the ethnographer, located in different settings.

Hammersley and Atkinson further suggest that to maximize the results of triangulation, the observers should be as different as possible and should have different roles in the field (231). I will return to this point in the discussion on teamwork in chapter 4. Hammersley and Atkinson note, however, that investigator triangulation does not usually occur, even when ethnographers do team research, since team members collect information on different aspects of a setting. The data generated by different team members are intended to be complementary rather than to facilitate triangulation. This is not true for RAP.

Sometimes the term triangulation is used to describe the combination or mixing of qualitative and quantitative research (Flick 1992, 177). This is *not* how the term is used in connection with RAP.

Hammersley and Atkinson (1995, 232) caution that simply aggregating more and more data does not necessarily produce a more complete picture. They suggest that having different types of data may be more important than the quantity of data:

What is involved in triangulation is not the combination of different kinds of data *per se*, but rather an attempt to relate different sorts of data in such a way as to counteract various possible threats to the validity of our analysis. (232)

Because different triangulation sources are recognized as having different strengths and weaknesses, they are picked to complement each other (Huberman and Miles 1994, 438).

While most social scientists are comfortable using the metaphor of triangulation, Richardson (1994) would like to see it replaced with "crystallization." According to her, triangulation assumes that there is a "fixed point" or "object" that can be triangulated. She rejects the notion that there can be a single, or triangulated, truth. She suggests that crystals are prisms that reflect the external and their refraction creates different colors and patterns. "What we see depends upon our angle of repose" (522). According to Richardson, crystallization provides us with a deepened, complex, but partial understanding of the topic. "Paradoxically, we know more and doubt what we know" (522). It seems to me that use of the term "crystallization" might help prevent us from thinking of triangulation in a mechanical way.

Triangulation and RAP

The example of the interview with the director of the not-for-profit organization illustrates triangulation using a multidisciplinary team of investigators, combining direct observations with semistructured interviewing, and combining information collected in advance with the interview process. It also illustrates the power of teamwork for triangulation. The synergy resulting from triangulation based on intensive teamwork is absolutely crucial for RAP.

When applied to RAP, the multidisciplinary team works together to collect data through semistructured interviews, through observations, and from information collected in advance of the RAP. Additional triangulation results from the different perceptions, theories, methods, and academic disciplines of the different team members (including the insiders on the team). The assumption is that for most situations there is no one best way to obtain information and that, even if there were, it could not be known in advance. Successful triangulation for RAP depends upon conscious selection of team members who can bring different perspectives, research techniques, theories, and disciplinary backgrounds. It then depends upon the team aggressively pursuing data from different sources. The issue of the selection of team members will be considered below in the section on Team Membership, p. 24.

Intensive team interaction as an element of triangulation (along with team interaction for the iterative analysis and additional collection of data) permits the RAP team to significantly reduce the time in the field. The lone researcher may require a prolonged period to triangulate a single piece of information using only two sources of information. Given the difficulty of both listening to others and collecting information on the physical context, while at the same time recording the information, the lone researcher may be forced to approach these sequentially. Without team interaction, a team of three researchers might be expected to require even longer (when the time of the individuals is added together) to collect the same information as the lone researcher. Working by themselves they still face the difficulty of focusing on several sources of data at the same time. There might be an increase in the triangulation with the greater number of observers, but even this is not certain, since without team interaction team members may not know the lines of inquiry or observations of the other team members.

Intensive team interaction is essential for triangulation for RAP.

When these same individuals interact with each other during the research time, tasks can be coordinated and shared. While one member leads the interview, another may assume responsibility for taking notes or recording the interview. At the same time, this team member may be observing for visual context and listening to the answers of the respondent from a different perspective based on different technical expertise. The communication between the team members, either directly or through their interaction with the respondent, provides immediate help and feedback to the other team member. The relationships that might take a lone researcher a significant amount of time to recognize may be revealed immediately and serve for new lines of inquiry. These in turn can result in additional cycles of triangulation. The possibility of triangulation based on different pieces of information and different interpretation of the same piece of information has suddenly multiplied many times. If team members are of different ages, gender, or ethnic identity, the potential for triangulation increases exponentially.

The presence of several team members makes it possible to collect more information per unit of time than can be collected by a lone researcher. The collection of additional information, however, is *not* the source of the strength resulting from the use of a team for RAP. The strength results from the team interaction and the impact of this interaction on the ability of the team to carry out triangulation at a very rapid rate.

Team interaction also has the potential for increasing the efficiency of data collection by allowing better decisions on what information is really needed. The observation of a team member that a certain line of inquiry may not be relevant has the potential of saving both data collection time and data analysis time. The assumption is that two heads are better than one, especially if the one is preoccupied with carrying on an interview or collecting some other information. The improved on-the-spot decision making concerning the information to be collected is in addition to the improvements in choices concerning data collection resulting from the iterative analysis and additional data collection.

Illustrative Research Techniques Associated with Triangulation

Team Membership

Multidisciplinary

> The disciplinary specialization of each team member usually is not as important as having different disciplines represented on the team.

By definition, RAP cannot be done by one person. The expertise brought to the situation by the team members and their willingness to work closely together may be the most critical components of RAP. Team members are chosen based on the specific situation being investigated and the availability of different individuals to serve on the team. Team members should represent a range of disciplines that are most relevant to the topic. For example, a RAP team investigating health practices might include a social worker, a medical doctor, a traditional healer, and a public administration specialist. An agricultural development RAP team might include an agricultural economist and an agronomist. The mix of specific disciplines on the team often is not as critical as having different disciplines represented. It is important for team members to understand the rationale for a team effort; explicit discussion of what different disciplines are expected to contribute to the team effort can be useful. The selection of team members and getting the team to work together are two of the most important responsibilities of the team leader. These issues are discussed in the section on Team Leadership, p. 94.

Diversity

Since one of the keys to RAP is the use of a team composed of individuals who are looking for different things, listening for different answers, remembering and putting together different information, and relating to the respondents in different ways, diversity on the team is extremely valuable. It should not be assumed that, just because individuals have different academic disciplines, they will bring the diversity in perceptions, theories, and methods needed. If this type of information is not already known, potential team members should be asked about it while the team is being assembled. While the specific situation being investigated will influence the types of diversity that are most relevant, age, gender, and ethnic identity should be considered.

Insiders/Outsiders

> **The RAP team should include a mix of insiders and outsiders.**

Teams should be composed of a mix of insiders from and outsiders to the situation being investigated. Outsiders are able to share experience and knowledge from other situations and their participation can be extremely valuable to the insiders in identifying options and in noting constraints that might otherwise be overlooked. At the same time, outsiders gain insights and knowledge from insiders that can guide their understanding of other situations they might investigate in the future. See Outsiders and Insiders, p. 89, for more information on the role of the insiders on the RAP team (also see Local Team Members, p. 118). Participation of insiders as full team members is one way of putting people first. Chambers notes that

> Where people and their wishes and priorities are not put first, projects that affect and involve them encounter problems. Experience shows that where people are consulted, where they participate freely, where their needs and priorities are given primacy in project identification, design, implementation, and monitoring, then economic and social performance are better and development is more sustainable. (1991, 515)

Small vs. Large Teams

RAP requires a minimum of two team members. Once the minimum requirements for disciplines and diversity have been reached, smaller teams of four or five members are preferred to larger teams. Members of large teams are more likely to engage in team interaction not related to triangulation, often just talking to one another, and are less likely to use team interaction to guide listening to and learning from others than are members of small teams. Large teams often intimidate respondents, are more likely to be conservative and cautious, and take longer to produce a report and recommendations (Chambers 1983, 23).

Team Interviewing

Semistructured interviews, whether with individuals or groups, provide numerous opportunities for triangulation, as team members representing different disciplines initiate varied lines of inquiry and raise issues that otherwise could be overlooked. Two related issues concerning team interviewing should be noted. First, the individual or group being interviewed must not feel that a gang of tag-team interviewers is attacking them. A brief explanation for the presence of a team instead of an individual interviewer may be appropriate. Deliberate pacing of the interview, with increased efforts to maintain a conversational tone, may be needed. As discussed in chapter 4, the team needs to be sensitive to the fact that there are some situations where the interview cannot be done by a team, either because of the respondent's general discomfort with a group or because of the nature of the topic. In these situations, one member of the team should do the interview. Second, team members must feel comfortable working together. This requires carefully listening to the questions by other team members and politely interrupting when appropriate. Conversely, team members must be comfortable being interrupted. A brief practice session with team interviewing may be useful. Careful reviews by the team following the first several actual group interviews will help everyone understand the specific behaviors that will be most beneficial. Prior agreement by the team on which team members will take the lead on specific topics is useful, but should not be interpreted as assigning topics exclusively to only one person. Conducting an interview requires the active participation of all team members. Intensive team interviewing is not based on sequential interviewing by members of the team, but on joint interviewing.

Team Observing

Direct observation is an important rapid assessment tool for validating data collected in advance, providing multiple checks on data collected from interviews, and suggesting additional topics for interviews. Direct observation can prevent RAP from being misled by myth (Chambers 1980, 12). "Try it yourself" is an abbreviated form of **participant observation** in which team members undertake an activity themselves. Doing so allows insights and prompts the volunteering of information that otherwise might not be accessible (Chambers 1991, 524). Depending upon the situation, several specific direct observation techniques have been found useful. Where locally accepted, a camera can be an extremely important research tool. Photos can be used to document conditions before an intervention. The preparation of sketch maps provides powerful visual tools that encourage the RAP team and local people to view community issues from a spatial perspective (see Mapping, p. 52). The use of proxy or unobtrusive indicators, such as the presence of drug paraphernalia, a sewing machine in a rural household, or changes in the construction materials for roofs, can provide insights about conditions and changes, especially when the local participants identify these indicators as relevant (see Unobtrusive Observations, p. 49).

Team Collection of Information

Combining information gathered from semistructured interviews and observations with that collected in advance provides RAP with some of the methodological strength usually associated with traditional qualitative approaches. Chambers (1980, 8) notes that despite the wealth of information in archives, including annual reports, reports of surveys, academic papers, and government statistics, rapid research teams often ignore these sources of data. The failure to collect basic data in advance of the RAP means that field research time is wasted in collecting already available data. Moreover, important research leads and topics suggested by previously collected material may be missed. The structure of the RAP process makes certain types of information collected in advance especially relevant. For example, minutes of past board meetings are particularly relevant to an investigation of a not-for-profit organization, while maps and aerial photos may be relevant for a team looking at community activities.

A team effort at collecting information in advance uses the varying expertise of the different team members to identify information that will be most relevant. This increases the chances that the needed information will be available to the team. The availability of the information improves the efficiency of the team in identifying topics of inquiry and increases the opportunity for triangulation resulting from the information collected in advance and the information collected during the fieldwork (see Materials Collected in Advance, p. 118).

Data Collection to Get the Insider's Perspective

A RAP is based on what the participants in the situation under investigation believe are the critical elements, the relative importance of these elements, and how they relate to each other. RAP is designed to elicit the insider's perspective, an objective shared with ethnography. RAP and ethnography share many characteristics and specific research techniques. The most significant difference between RAP and ethnography is RAP's use of intensive teamwork to substitute for the prolonged fieldwork normally associated with ethnography. RAP does not reject or abandon the traditional methods and techniques of the social sciences, but provides for ways to complement and enrich them.

There is no universally accepted definition for ethnography (Ely et al., 1991, 4; Lincoln and Guba 1985, 8). There are, however, significant areas of agreement between most definitions, and these areas of agreement suggest that RAP and ethnography are similar. Ethnography is qualitative research. Since several of the characteristics of qualitative research are especially relevant to RAP, a brief examination of qualitative research will contribute to a better understanding of RAP.

> Qualitative research/ethnographic research (1) helps define for RAP what it means to get at the insider's perspective and (2) provides research techniques.

Qualitative Research

Sherman and Webb have identified five characteristics shared by all qualitative research:

1. Events can be understood adequately only if they are seen in context.

2. Nothing is predefined or taken for granted.

3. Participants need to speak for themselves. For participants to be able to speak for themselves, there is a need for an interactive process between the persons studied and the researcher.

4. The aim of qualitative research is to understand the whole experience.

5. There is not one method and choices are made based on appropriateness. (1988, 5–8)

Sherman and Webb focus on the importance of the perceptions of the participants in their much-quoted definition: "Qualitative research, then, has the aim of understanding experience as nearly as possible as its participants feel it or live it" (7). Denzin and Lincoln also emphasize the perspective of the people studied in their statement that "qualitative researchers study things in their natural settings, attempting to make sense of or interpret phenomena in terms of the meaning people bring to them" (1994, 2). Miles and Huberman note that the researcher attempts to capture the perceptions "from the inside," through a process of "deep attentiveness, of empathetic understanding" and that this requires the researcher to suspend preconceptions about the topics under investigation (1994, 6). They argue that "a main task is to explicate the ways people in particular settings come to understand, account for, take action, and otherwise manage their day-to-day situations" (7). Creswell (1998, 14) attempts to summarize common characteristics of qualitative research described by several leading authors on the subject. He suggests that these authors agree that qualitative research is conducted in a natural setting where the researcher is an instrument of data collection, that data analysis begins with observation of particulars and then moves to the development of general hypotheses, and that the focus is on the interpretation of meaning by the participants.

Two other characteristics of qualitative research are especially relevant to RAP and need to be embraced by RAP team members. First, all social science research involves a trade-off between the number of cases investigated and the number of variables examined for each case. Qualitative research is based on a few cases and many variables whereas quantitative research works with a few variables and many cases (Ragin 1987 as cited in Creswell 1998, 15–16). When the objective is to understand the perspective of the insiders with special attention to understanding their categories, fewer cases covered in depth are preferred to more cases covered in less depth. Second, qualitative research assumes there will be ambiguity. Qualitative researchers cannot know what they will learn and must be able to tolerate uncertainty (Ely et al. 1991, 135). They also need to recognize that what they find may not have one clear meaning. Results are often ambiguous. The RAP team should practice the mantra "I can live with ambiguity" until they believe it.

The RAP mantra: "I can live with ambiguity."

Ethnography

The numerous approaches to qualitative research (see Creswell 1998, 6) reflect different disciplines and are based on different procedures for data collection and analysis, and the production of reports. It is not always clear what differentiates one approach from another and there is little agreement on even the number of different approaches. Studies can be based on a combination of different approaches. There is, however, general consensus that ethnography is an approach to qualitative research that is especially concerned with description.

While I especially like the statement by Spradley and McCurdy that "ethnography is based on learning from people as opposed to studying people" (1972, 12), it does not differentiate ethnography from other qualitative research. Miles and Huberman (1994, 8) describe ethnography as based on extended contact with a given community, concerned with the mundane, day-to-day events as well as the unusual ones, and involving direct or indirect participation in local activities. For them, the focus of ethnography is on the description of local particularities and the individual's perspectives and interpretations of their world. Wolcott's (1987) definition of ethnography as a study of an intact cultural or social group or an individual or individuals within the group based primarily on observation introduces the important concept of cultural group. The extensive reference to cultural groups and culture help differentiate ethnography from other qualitative research.

Ethnographic methods are descriptive; the two principal means of collecting data are participant observation and semistructured interviews. Sometimes documents are also collected. The ethnographer listens to informants and records their voices with the intent of generating a cultural portrait (Wolcott 1987). The analyst's task is to "reach across multiple data sources" (including but not limited to observations, interviews, artifacts, and documents) and "to condense them" (Miles and Huberman 1994, 8). Miles and Huberman suggest that ethnographers do this with less concern for conceptual or theoretical meaning of the observations than some other qualitative researchers. Bernard concedes that in the past anthropologists were mostly concerned with description, but that today many anthropologists "are interested in research questions that demand explanation and prediction" (1995, 176).

Almost all descriptions of ethnography refer to a requirement for prolonged periods in the field, often defined as twelve months or more (Bernard 1995; Creswell 1998; Miles and Huberman 1994; Wolcott 1987, 1995). This topic will be discussed in more detail in chapter 5, when I consider the arguments by some anthropologists that a RAP is too quick to be ethnographic research. Despite the widespread identification of ethnography with prolonged fieldwork, there are occasional references to the possibility that ethnography can be done in less time. In addition to the researchers discussed in chapter 8 associated with rapid ethnographic research (Robert Redfield and Sol Tax, James Spradley and

David McCurdy, and Penn Handwerker), Margaret Mead is described as being neither bashful nor apologetic about the short duration of her fieldwork experiences (Wolcott 1995, 78).

There are some situations where prolonged fieldwork is required to gain access and build rapport. There are other situations involving events that unfold slowly, like agricultural cycles or the merger of organizations, where prolonged fieldwork is necessary. However, for most situations, RAP should produce a sufficiently rich understanding of the insider's perspective to initiate interventions that need to be started quickly or to design additional research.

Culture

The generation of a cultural portrait has been identified as one of the purposes for ethnography. The words "cultural" and "culture" have special meaning when used by qualitative researchers and these meanings have implications for RAP. Some social scientists have defined culture as nearly everything that has been learned or produced by a group of people. A more limited definition proposed by Spradley and McCurdy (1972) restricts the concept of culture to the knowledge people use to generate and interpret social behavior. This knowledge is learned and, to a degree, is shared. Spradley and McCurdy note that this definition can have an extremely significant influence on research: "It shifts the focus of research from the perspective of the ethnographer as an outsider to a discoverer of the insider's point of view" (9). The task of the researcher is not to discover everything that a group of people has learned, but to discover the insider's perspective on the shared knowledge people use for social behavior. Since culture is learned, and since we all learn different things, no two people can have identical cultural configurations. This also means that any one person will have different cultural configurations at different points in his or her life. The fact that culture is learned and shared, but that each individual participates in different groups where she/he learns different things, means that everyone participates in many cultures. Finally, all cultures are dynamic. Disagreements among local people as to what are the significant categories, or even the words they use for these categories, should be expected.

Emic and Etic

One of the goals for qualitative research, including ethnography and RAP, is to understand the categories the local people use for dividing up their reality and identifying the terms they use for these categories. The categories used by the local people are referred to as "**emic**" and the categories used by the researcher, if he or she is an outsider, are referred to as "**etic**." When I was a graduate student, these terms were illustrated with the following example. The first situation illustrates an etic approach. If I am interested in the way a group describes the colors of objects, I could start by pointing to an object that is dark green and then inquire about the word they use. I have started with my classification of colors, where there is a discrete category for dark green, and it is unlikely I will discover that their categories for colors, the way they divide colors, is different from my categories. An emic approach would be to suspend for a moment my classification system and to start by trying to understand their categories. I might present a color wheel where there are no divisions between the different shades and ask the respondent to provide the boundaries and to then provide labels. I could also start with a color photograph or natural objects and collect information on colors. Using this approach, I would discover that several groups in southern Sudan have only one category that includes dark green and black and only use one term to describe them. Closer to home, the emic system used by students in an American high school will be found to have numerous categories for their classmates, including categories of "wannabes." It quickly becomes obvious that a given student could fit into numerous categories and that different students, even though they share in a similar culture, will identify slightly different classification systems.

The following summary of an "emic" approach is based on Pelto and Pelto (1978, 62):

1. Primary method is interviewing, in-depth and in the local language.

2. Intent is to seek the categories of meaning, as nearly as possible in the ways the locals define things.

3. The people's definitions of meaning, their idea systems, are seen as the most important causes or explanations of behavior.

4. Systems and patterns are identified through logical analysis.

5. The methodology begins with particular observations and uses them as a foundation for understanding, since research cannot proceed until the local categories of meaning have been discovered.

Two points of caution are necessary. No one waits to identify all of the local categories before beginning to discuss issues or ask questions. The assumption has to be that some of the outsiders' definitions are useful. The goal is to be sensitive to the possibility that the categories of the insiders may not be the same as the categories of the outsiders and, where appropriate, to try to elicit the emic categories. The second point is that communication about the local situation may require that emic categories be translated into etic ones that can be understood. An excellent study on fire-wood/energy use in northern Sudan made extensive use of emic categories. The local people use a "donkey" load as their unit of measurement. The author of the study also referred to donkey loads in her report without defining the term, and consequently some of her most important research findings were essentially useless to the rest of the world.

Indigenous Knowledge

The beginning point for understanding complex local situations has to be the understanding of the local participants. The goal of RAP is to construct a model of the local situation consistent with the way local people understand it. Doing so usually means trying to use local categories for dividing and describing reality. Using indigenous knowledge involves seeking agreement on the most important problems or constraints faced by the local participants (Galt, 1987). Indigenous knowledge of local systems cannot capture the totality of these situations and there will always be areas where local understanding of reality is limited. The involvement of outsiders on the RAP team can help move the understanding of the situation beyond that possible by the local participants. At the same time, the outsiders will desperately need the continuous input of the local participants to avoid serious errors understanding the situation (Galt, 1987).

Variability

One of the tasks of the ethnographic research is to recognize and seek out variability and not to focus exclusively on the "average." In many situations, the average student, small businessperson, farmer, or health-care administrator exists only as an artifact of statistics. If the average weight is defined as a ten-pound range for children of a specific age, it might be found that 30 percent of children are average. If the average height is defined as a five-inch range, it might also be found that 30 percent of children are average. However, if both height and weight are used, the number of children who are average will be far less than 30 percent, because not everyone with an "average" height will also have an "average" weight. Each time, an additional variable is used to define the average, fewer and fewer actual cases of the "average" can be found. Eventually, enough variables are used to define the average that almost no one is left who is average. In many situations, variability and distributions of characteristics are more important than the "average." Qualitative research approaches that focus on the average or are implemented with inadequate time in the field are especially prone to ignore variability. Ignoring variability can be dangerous when it results in the development of interventions that the "average" recipients are expected passively to adopt. Recognition of variability can be an important beginning point for developing interventions that provide people with expanded options and that respect their ability to chose among them (Beebe 1994).

Illustrative Research Techniques Associated with Ethnography

Semistructured Interviews

Semistructured interviews based on guidelines are the key to RAP. The most important way of learning about local conditions is to ask local people what they know. The goal is to get people to talk on a subject and not just answer questions. Sufficient time must be invested to establish a rapport and to explain the purpose of the RAP.

Semistructured interviews are the key to RAP.

The interview should be a dialogue or process in which important information develops out of casual conversation. Metzler defines a creative interview as, "a two-person conversational *exchange* of information on behalf of an unseen audience to produce a level of enlightenment neither participant could produce alone" (1997, 12). The key to successful informal interviewing is to be natural and relaxed while guiding the conversation to a fruitful end. *"Talk with people and listen to their concerns and views"* (Rhoades 1982, 17). Metzler suggests that "if you want candor—you want human responses rather than defensive exaggerations and false facades—try revealing a little of yourself in the conversation." He also suggests that striving for technical perfection can intrude on candor and that it is better to just have people talking (Metzler 1997, 2).

It is important to avoid the opinion poll syndrome, in which the RAP team drives up and jumps out with clipboards in hand, ready to interview. The RAP team needs to be especially sensitive to the fact that people may be suspicious of outsiders (Rhoades 1987, 119–120). The team needs to recognize that the time of the respondents is valuable and it needs to be able to accommodate the respondents' schedules. Because the assumption is that a RAP is based on collaboration between the local people and the team, payment for interviews is usually inappropriate. However, expression of appreciation, including symbolic small gifts, may be very appropriate.

The semistructured interview is flexible, but it is also controlled (Burgess 1982, 107). This type of interviewing has also been called "conversation with a purpose" (Webb and Webb 1932, 130). It has been suggested that the RAP must keep respondents relating experiences and attitudes that are relevant to the problem, and encourage them to discuss these experiences naturally and freely.

Experience has suggested that there are specific things that will improve an interview. Open the interview with a "Grand Tour" question (Spradley 1979). Such a question might be "So tell me something about yourself" or "How did you happen to get here?" I knew I had found a good "Grand Tour" question when I asked one of the state farm managers in Poland to tell me about his farm. He replied by telling me that at the end of the last ice age, as the glaciers melted, they left different types of soils in different places on his farm. I expected to be there a long time with that opening! It turned out this was relevant information for the types of enterprises on this farm.

Wolcott (1995, 111) suggests becoming an active and creative listener. This means more than being an attentive listener. It means using the listening to better play an interactive role and thereby make a more effective speaker out of the person talking. Other ways of improving interviews include the use of culturally appropriate nonverbal behavior, such as paralanguage, voice, and eye contact (Metzler 1997, 52–53). The grunts and noises an interviewer makes in response to comments—the "umms," "uh-huhs," and "mmmmms"—are called paralanguage (52). Studies on the effects of these sounds leave no doubt that they contribute to the rapport. People speak longer when they hear those kinds of responses. The tone of voice carries subtle but effective meaning. Experiments suggest that when words clash with the tone of voice and facial expression, people tend to believe the nonverbal aspects. Various studies suggest that eye contact enhances response and that people tend to look at the other person more while listening than while talking. However, it should be noted that in some cultures eye contact, especially between people who are not well known to each other, is considered rude.

One of the keys to successful interviewing is learning how to probe effectively, "that is, to stimulate an informant to produce more information, without injecting yourself so much into the interaction that you only get a reflection of yourself in the data" (Bernard 1995, 215). Sometimes it is necessary to repeat a question, which should be done without expanding or elaborating. When you expand or elaborate you are likely to suggest an answer or to change the question (Wolcott 1995, 112). Depending on the culture, one of the most effective and difficult to learn probes is the silent probe. It consists of just remaining quiet and waiting for an informant to continue. Ely et al. note that it may be especially difficult to remain silent, and thus let the respondent continue, when what is said strikes a chord with the interviewer and he or she feels compelled to share because, after all, "we've been there." (1991, 60). Interviewers are reminded to distinguish between a pregnant pause and dead silence (Wolcott 1995, 111). Another kind of probe consists of simply repeating the last thing an informant has said and asking them to continue. This probe may be especially useful when an informant is describing a process, or an event (216).

Keeping the interview moving naturally requires a few comments and remarks, together with an occasional question designed to keep the subject on the main theme, to secure more details, and to stimulate the conversation when it lags. Examples of nondirective probes include:

> Give me a description of. . . .
> Tell me what goes on when you. . . .
> Describe what it's like to. . . .
> Tell me about. . . . Tell me more about that. . . .
> Let's see [pause]. I'm having trouble figuring out how I can word this.
> Give me an example.
> How might someone do that?
> How important is that concern?
> So, the message you want me to get from that story is. . . .
> Say more.
> Keep talking.
> Don't stop.
> How come your energy level just went down?
> What am I not asking? (adopted from Market Navigation 2000)

RAP team members need to have understanding and sympathy for the informant's point of view. "They need to follow their informants' responses and to listen to them carefully in order that a decision can be made concerning the direction in which to take the interview. In short, researchers have to be able to share the culture of their informants" (Burgess 1982, 108).

There are techniques for "jogging" respondents' memories that will improve the accuracy of their responses. When time has passed since the events being discussed, respondents can be asked to begin by recalling personal landmarks. Once the list of personal landmark events is established, it may be easier to recall other events in relation to them (Bernard 1995, 235). While there are several specific techniques that can be used to help deal with memory errors, the one I believe is most relevant to RAP is asking respondents to consult records, such as bank statements, telephone bills, and minutes of meetings. Often, copies of these documents can be requested.

Direct quotes are critical for telling the story of the local participants. In reports, direct quotes can be used to establish authority and authenticity. Direct quotes employing idiosyncratic speech, figures of speech, metaphors, and local sayings add human color. Even when these quotes are in English, they may need to be translated. The really good quotes that meet these needs may not occur spontaneously. Journalists have developed techniques that can facilitate this process and are relevant to ethnographic interviews.

Metzler suggests several techniques for encouraging people to talk more "quotably" (1997, 102). He suggests asking for a simile or an analogy. The question is "What is it like to . . . ?" The inclusion of metaphors in questions or comments will often elicit responses that include metaphors. However, if the respondent uses your metaphor in the response, it is not authentically his or hers, and another probe may be necessary. Other ways of getting rich responses are to use questions like:

> Is there an old Texas (substitute local place) saying that covers this situation?
>
> Can you put a label on this for me?
>
> How would you explain this to your nine-year-old daughter?
>
> The situation you describe sounds like a sophisticated Monopoly game—are you winning or losing? (104–105)

Sometimes respondents or informants will telegraph a quote. There is a need to be especially attentive when you hear phrases like "In my view" and "Long years of experience have prompted me to suggest" (105).

Metzler (1997, 106) suggests that dramatically showing your appreciation for a quotable remark can encourage the respondent to produce more since they now know you are looking for them. He also suggests that the interviewer needs to stay particularly alert for personal asides. These can differ significantly in content and style from the more structured responses provided in response to semistructured questions.

As a general rule, interviews should be conducted under conditions most relevant to and revealing about the local system being investigated. For example, a RAP on health care should include interviews in the clinics where services are provided, while a RAP on agriculture should include interviews in farmers' fields, where the team can witness farmers' behavior. If the interviews with the farmers in the western Sudanese village had not occurred in their fields, it is unlikely that the role trees that harbor birds play in decisions on crop rotation would have ever surfaced. Actual observation permits the identification of new topics for discussion. Conducting as many interviews as possible at the site of the action being investigated is an important part of observation (see Participant Observation, p. 48). The RAP team should always note where interviews were conducted.

The RAP team needs to be aware that the answers they get can be influenced by numerous factors. In many cases, there is little that the team can do about these, other than to be aware that they exist and to be cautious about the answers. Different people asking the same question will sometimes get different answers, and even the same person asking the same question but in different settings may get different answers. Factors that influence responses include race, sex, age, and accent of both the interviewer and the respondent; the source of funding for a project; the level of experience of the interviewer; cultural norms about talking to strangers; and whether the question is controversial or not (Bernard 1995, 230). In many cultures, women get different responses to questions than men.

Sometimes informants will tell you what they think you want to know, in order not to offend you. The way questions are worded can make a difference in the answers you get, especially for more threatening questions (Bernard 1995, 232). It is possible to get the results you expect, not simply because you have correctly anticipated things, but because you have helped to shape the responses merely by the RAP team's presence. For example, the presence of a RAP team listening carefully to the concerns of local people can impact their views as to whether anyone is interested in their problems and thus whether they should try to influence things. It is also possible to see "what you want to see, even when it's not there"(233).

Use of Short Guidelines

The disagreement among ethnographers over the extent to which they should develop hypotheses and detailed guidelines before starting their work extends to RAP. Some RAP teams begin with pages of detailed guidelines that are to be followed closely, with all questions being asked. At the other extreme, some RAP teams begin with only a brief list of topics. Failure to offer specific questions appears to be premised on the belief that interviews should be very general and wide-ranging, especially since the team is exploring, and searching for an unknown number of elements. It is claimed that a framework prepared before beginning a RAP can predispose team members toward their own ideas, thereby blocking opportunities to gain new insights.

My experience suggests that short guidelines prepared in advance can be useful as long as they are not relied on too much. "In this early phase, the researcher is like an explorer, making a rapid survey of the horizon before plunging into the thickets from which the wider view is no longer possible" (Rhoades 1982, 5). While one may begin with guidelines, important questions and the direction of the study emerge as information is collected. Interviews should be planned around a few big issues. The interview then focuses on exploring the dimensions of an issue instead of details from a long list of questions (Wolcott 1995, 112). Bernard (1995, 217) suggests you can get longer responses by making your questions longer. Instead of asking sponge divers "What is it like to make a dive into very deep water?" ask "Tell me about diving into really deep water. What do you do to get ready and how do you descend and ascend? What's it like down there?" While Bernard notes that asking longer questions does not necessarily produce better responses, they are likely to keep informants talking and "the more you can keep an informant talking, the more you can express interest in what they are saying and the more you build rapport" (217).

Guidelines should not be viewed as an agenda to be diligently worked through, but as an aid to memory and a reminder of what might be missed (Bottrall 1981, 248 in Chambers 1983, 25). "Not everything needs to be known. The key . . . is to move quickly and surely to the main problems, opportunities, and actions" (Chambers 1983, 25).

> **The goal of RAP is to have people tell their stories and not to have them answer your questions.**

Use of a Tape Recorder

Bernard (1995, 222) cautions against relying on your memory in interviewing and recommends using a tape recorder in all cases except where respondents specifically ask you not to. He notes that, even when there are no plans to transcribe interviews, tapes can be used to fill in missing information from notes taken during the interview (223). Both Patton (1990, 350–351) and Bernard (1995, 223) provide specific advice on the choice and use of equipment. Sometimes they provide conflicting advice. The following is adapted from these sources, supplemented from my experience. What works for Patton, Bernard, or Beebe may not work for you, so you should practice until you have identified what does.

- Better two relatively small, inexpensive tape recorders than one expensive recorder. Use two tape recorders at the same time or keep the second one with you as a spare. At a minimum, you need a recorder that has a tape counter (for keeping up with where you are on the tape, both as you record and as you transcribe) and jacks for "remote," an external microphone, and earphones. Voice-activated features are not needed and should not be used. I like machines that use standard-size tapes so the tapes can be used with almost any machine.

- You need an inexpensive foot pedal (less than about $5.00) that plugs into the "remote" jack on the recorder and allows you to start and stop the machine. Machines that allow you to rewind using the foot pedal are called transcription machines and can cost many times more than a regular recorder.

- You will need comfortable earphones for transcribing.

- Always start with fresh batteries and have extra batteries with you. I have found it easier and more reliable to use batteries than to rely on outlets.

- Use high-quality tapes, the kind put together with screws that can be opened when the tape tangles.

- Use tapes identified as "90" or less. A "90" tape provides forty-five minutes of time on each side. Longer tapes are thinner and more subject to stretching.

- Always take along extra tape cassettes.

- Test the system before going to the interview. Test the system again at the interview.

- Set the recorder on a stable surface.

- Test the system again, but this time with the respondent talking. The respondent can be asked to give the date, time, location, their name, and the names of the interviewers. Where literacy is an issue, have the respondent record their informed consent. Then rewind the tape and play it back so the respondent can hear whether she/he is speaking distinctly.

- Immediately after removing the tape from the machine, label it, break out the small plastic tabs on the bottom of the cassette, and return the tape to an appropriate container. Breaking out the tabs is very important, since this prevents accidentally erasing or taping over material. These accidents are most likely while transcribing. When you are ready to use the tape for another purpose, you can use cellophane tape to cover the small holes where the plastic tabs were.

Experience teaches that equipment will fail, so you need to take extra precautions, have backups, and be prepared for the backups also to fail (see Interview Notes in Addition to Recording, p. 122).

> NEVER substitute tape recording for note taking.

Never substitute tape for note taking. A lot of very bad things can happen to tape, and if you haven't got back-up notes, you're out of luck. Don't wait until you get home to take notes, either. Take notes during the interview *about* the interview. (Bernard 1995, 223)

Use of Interpreters

Many qualitative researchers subscribe to the hypothesis that human beings speaking different languages live in different worlds, with language acting as filters on reality and molding perceptions of the worlds (Werner and Campbell 1970, 398). Ideally, all members of a RAP team should speak the language of the people from the situation being investigated. In practice, however, one or more members of a team may not speak the local language and an interpreter must be used. There is no excuse for failing to learn and use appropriate greetings. Knowledge of numbers and even a very few key words can allow a team member to appear to understand more than he or she actually does. This can improve rapport and the quality of the translation. Interpreters should be chosen carefully to ensure that they understand technical words that are likely to be used in the questions or answers. Werner and Campbell (1970) suggest that interpreters be chosen on the basis of their competence in the target language rather than in English. Before the interview, the team should go over the interview strategy with the interpreter, emphasizing that the team is interested in more than just "answers" to "questions." Werner and Campbell suggest providing the interpreter with a reformulated English version of the interview guidelines. They identify the following steps for the preparation of this reformulated version:

1. Get a good dictionary and a good thesaurus of English.

2. Rewrite all complex sentences as simple sentences.

3. Eliminate all metaphors and idioms.

4. Look up all the key words in the simple sentences and include two sets of possible paraphrases for each sentence: (a) paraphrases which are acceptable and (b) paraphrases which are not. The researcher presents the interpreter with both sets and explains that translations should be close to the acceptable paraphrases. (408–409)

The interpreter should not be physically between the speaker and the person being interviewed, but rather beside or slightly behind so that his or her function is clearly indicated. The team member should speak in brief sentences using a minimum number of words to express complete thoughts. The interpreter should be given time to translate before proceeding to the next thought. The team member should talk directly to the respondent, as if the respondent can understand everything said (Bostain 1970, 1). It is especially important to record interviews where an interpreter has been used, since this permits the translation to be checked.

Selection of Respondents

In most situations people can be interviewed about their own experience or their knowledge of the broader system beyond their own experience. Differentiating between these types of interviews can result in better information. Persons interviewed about their experience are referred to as **individual respondents**. They should be selected to represent variability. It should be clear to both the respondent and team members asking the questions that the questions concern only the individual's knowledge and behavior, and not what he or she thinks about the knowledge and behavior of others. Persons interviewed about the broader system are referred to as **key informants** and should be selected because of their experience and knowledge. Unless the terms "informants" or "respondents" are modified with the words "individual" or "key," they can be used interchangeably. "Participants" is another term that is used interchangeably with "respondents" and "informants" to identify the persons interviewed as part of the RAP process. The term "subjects" is generally not used.

Interviews should be conducted with an opportunity sample of purposely selected individual respondents. These individual respondents should be chosen because they represent a wide range of individuals in the situation being investigated and those chosen should not be limited to what is assumed to be representative or average. The research team for the Polish state farm study explicitly requested interviews with successful managers, unsuccessful managers, midlevel managers, a tractor driver, field workers, Ministry of Agriculture personnel, bankers, cooperative officials, and nonstate farmers. The RAP team needs to be sensitive to the bias that would be introduced if only one gender was interviewed when both are involved in a situation.

Seek out the trouble makers.

Following Honadle's (1979, 45) strategy for avoiding biases when investigating organizations, the RAP team could ask for the names of one or more individual respondents who are known to disagree with all decisions, generally promote trouble, and never cooperate with programs. Responses from these persons can provide valuable cross-checks and insights not available from other interviews.

Key informants are expected to be able to answer questions about the knowledge and behavior of others and especially about the operations of the broader environment. They are willing to talk and are assumed to have in-depth knowledge. Key informants for a study of a school system might include student leaders, administrators, school-board members, and leaders of parent-teacher associations. It is usually worthwhile to ask which people are most knowledgeable and then seek them out. Key informants may need to be interviewed several times with information from one session or information from other respondents identifying topics for the next session. The time constraints of a RAP should not be used as an excuse for not interviewing the same person several times if this is appropriate (see Follow-up Interviews with the Same Person, p. 123).

Individuals and Focus Groups

Focus group interviews where one or more team members moderate an interview with a group of respondents can be extremely useful in collecting certain types of information. The hallmark of focus groups is their explicit use of group interaction to produce data and insights that would be less accessible without the interaction found in a group. Morgan (1997, 2) defines focus groups as a research technique that collects data through group interaction on a topic determined by the researcher. In essence, it is the researcher's interest that provides the focus, whereas the data themselves come from the group interaction (6). Group interviews can be used in some cultures to collect information on topics where an individual may be penalized if he or she replies truthfully, but where a group talking about the community may not feel threatened (Chambers 1980, 14). Often, similar topics can be taken up in interviews with groups and "key informants." Group interviews where individuals are free to correct each other and discuss issues can identify variability within the community and prevent an atypical situation from being confused with the average.

My experience suggests that group interviews may reveal what people believe are preferred patterns as opposed to what actually exists. A very detailed description of the local crop rotation system by a group of farmers in the village in western Sudan was later found not to be practiced by any of them exactly as described (Beebe 1982). Even when some topics have been covered by a group interview, the same topics should still be covered with individuals. The question changes from "What do local people generally do?" to "What do you do?"

The presence of others often influences answers, and who is present during an interview may need to be noted. The presence of authority figures can almost always be expected to influence comments. For the western Sudan village study, about the only time the team was alone with individuals was during visits to their fields. The presence of neighbors and especially the village leader seemed to increase the number of positive comments about the government. The initial report that agriculture extension agents who had been useful had visited the village was not confirmed in the interviews with individuals. One participant remembered only one visit, some twenty-five years in the past, during which the extension agent had brought tree seeds that did not survive. In another individual interview, the participant suggested that the agriculture extension agents who had visited the village were useless and contrasted them to the technicians from the water department who had helped with a well in a nearby village.

Structured Interviews

Structured interviews involve the use of the same question asked of every informant. The most common form of structured interviewing is the questionnaire. In chapter 1, I noted that there is a role for questionnaire survey research, but that it is often not an appropriate beginning point for understanding complex situations, especially when local categories are not known. Prolonged fieldwork provides an opportunity for the creation of survey instruments after the local categories and words for these categories have been identified. Usually there is not sufficient time in a RAP to develop and administer a questionnaire that uses the categories and words of the local people. One purpose for doing a RAP is to build up enough of an understanding of a local situation to be able to develop a culturally relevant questionnaire. There are a few circumstances where structured questions may be appropriate as part of a RAP. When several individuals are going to be interviewed, structured questions on demographic variables, including age, gender, and residence, or concerning possessions or participation in events may be the most efficient way of collecting this information.

Comparing and Sorting Objects

Physical objects can be used as stimuli for eliciting responses. Objects can be three-by-five-inch index cards with names of people, places, or objects; photographs; or the actual objects, such as plants or birth control devices. In a triad test, three objects are presented and the respondent is asked to either identify the one that does not fit, choose the two that seem to go together, or choose the two that are the same. Discussion often centers on what the respondent thinks it means to be the "same" or to "fit together" (Bernard 1995, 244–245). In a pile sort, the respondent is asked to sort objects (often cards with the names of things or concepts written on them, although they could be photographs or physical objects) into piles, putting things that are similar together in a pile. Discussion can center on what is meant by "similar." If the respondent asks whether something can be put in more than one pile, Bernard (1995, 249) suggests three possible responses: saying "no" because there is one card per item and a card can only be in one pile at a time, making up a duplicate card on the spot, or asking the respondent to do multiple pile sorts of the same objects. These techniques have been extensively used for "cultural domain analysis." When these techniques are used as part of a RAP, the objective is not cultural domain analysis but to stimulate general discussion. Given the time constraints of RAP, the sophisticated analysis associated with cultural domain analysis would not be appropriate. In a RAP, these techniques are as likely to be administered to a group as to individuals.

Participant Observation

Pelto and Pelto observe that "every individual is a participant observer—if not of other cultures, then at least of one's own" (1978, 69). Participant observation as an essential ethnographic technique, however, requires much more than simply being there and passively watching. It requires systematically exploring relationships among different events and recording what is seen and heard. Ely et al. (1991) speak about intensive observing, listening, and speaking. Anthropologists generally recognize that the role of the participant-observer can range from full participant, defined as actually living and working in the field as a member of the group over an extended time, to mute observer. The essential requirements for participant observation are that people must feel comfortable with your presence and allow you to get close enough to observe (Bernard 1995, 136).

Interview where listening can be combined with observing.

In the section on semistructured interviewing (see Semistructured Interviews, p. 35, especially pp. 39–40), I emphasized that interviews need to be conducted in a relevant setting where listening can be combined with observing. I strongly agree with Ely et al. that "interviewing cannot be divorced from looking, interacting, and attending to more than the actual interview words" (1991, 43).

Even though there is not a lot of time during a RAP to do participant observation, there are more opportunities than one might expect. Every interview is an opportunity for participant observation and the results of every interview should include observations. There are sometimes opportunities to do things that are observed. My attempt to spread some fertilizer in a rice field in the Philippines was not very successful, but the comic relief it provided to the farmers resulted in some wonderful dialogue on how one learns new farming practices. The results of a "try it yourself" can significantly enhance the results of an interview. Finally, even during a RAP there are opportunities that should not be missed for sharing time outside the boundaries of interview sessions. Whenever possible, the RAP team should spend the night in the local setting. Critical events during the early mornings, evenings, or nights may not arise in interviews during office hours. Sharing of meals provides opportunities for informal discussions and follow up to topics discussed during formal interviews. If it is not possible to share meals, it is almost always possible to share tea or coffee. The RAP team needs to be especially sensitive about imposing on the hospitality of others and must be ready to return favors.

Unobtrusive Observations

Unobtrusive observations are direct observations done inconspicuously in which the participant may or may not be aware of the observation when it occurs. Often, physical objects are observed and used as proxy indicators for social behavior. "A well-worn path provides excellent, though incomplete, evidence concerning the volume of traffic between two communities; the different states of disrepair of buildings provide possible indexes of relative affluence; the extensiveness of refuse heaps give testimony to duration of occupation" (Pelto and Pelto 1978, 115). Other examples of unobtrusive observation include graffiti in public toilets, the age of automobiles in junkyards, and the presence of television satellite dishes or antennae in rural neighborhoods. The strength of these observations for a RAP is that they open new areas for discussion and for getting at the interpretations that local people provide of them. Unobtrusive observations are appropriate in public places where questions of privacy do not exist. Usually such observation is considered as having insignificant potential to harm participants. Fluehr-Lobban (1998, 184) notes that even if unobtrusive observation does not harm participants, this does not exempt researchers from providing full disclosure (see Team Observing, p. 27).

Folktales and Other Verbal Lore

Folktales, myths, songs, proverbs, riddles, and jokes can provide insights into local situations and interesting focal points around which to initiate discussion. As one of the objectives shared by ethnography and RAP is to get people to tell their stories, the possibility of asking people to literally tell stories should not be overlooked. Even a rough content analysis of verbal lore can suggest possible themes for subsequent examination. Variations in the same story as told by different individuals can provide evidence of the diffusion of information (Pelto and Pelto 1978, 113).

Systems, Soft Systems, and Rich Pictures

Even limited attention to systems methodology can provide an expanded set of conceptual tools and specific techniques for understanding how local people view their system. It should be noted, however, that the same techniques often are chosen by social scientists based on their professional training and experience without reference to "systems." A system can be defined as a set of mutually related elements that constitute a whole, having properties as an entity (Checkland and Scholes 1990, 4). For the purposes of RAP, it is useful to expand this definition to include the point that the elements in the system behave in a way that an observer has chosen to view as coordinated to accomplish one or more purposes (Wilson and Morren 1990, 70). A systems approach initially considers all aspects of a local situation, but quickly moves toward the definition of a model that focuses on only the most important elements and their relationships to each other. Systems are always complex, and it is not possible to deal with all aspects of a system at the same time. The first task of a RAP team is to make a rough approximation of the system and to identify the elements that are most important for the specific situation being examined. It is very important to note that the elements in a system usually cannot be identified in advance, nor can decisions be made in advance as to which elements of a system are most important for understanding a given situation.

Soft Systems Methodology is one approach to systems thinking that is especially relevant to RAP. Soft Systems Methodology is associated with Checkland, who has identified several specific steps:

1. identifying a situation which has provoked concern;

2. selecting some relevant human activity system;

3. making a model of the activity;

4. using the model to question the real-world situation; and

5. using the debate initiated by the comparison to define action which would improve the original problem situation. (Checkland and Scholes 1990)

Umans (1997, 11–13) used Soft Systems Methodology for program planning in a rapid appraisal of the traditional health knowledge system of the Guarani Indians in Bolivia. After the Soft Systems model of the role of traditional midwives was compared with the real-world situation, it was decided that independent supervision of midwives was not being done. After a discussion of this discrepancy, it was decided to include this in a list of proposals to improve the existing situation.

A critical element of Soft Systems Methodology is to develop a "**rich picture**" of the situation under investigation. Drawing diagrams and pictures allows both individuals and groups to express and check information in ways that are often more valid than talk. Checkland and Scholes (1990, 45) argue the reason for this "is that human affairs reveal a rich moving pageant of relationships, and pictures are a better means for recording relationships and connections." The rich picture is literally a drawing to which all the participants in the activity are encouraged to contribute. Figure 2.1 is an example of a rich picture from the not-for-profit RAP.

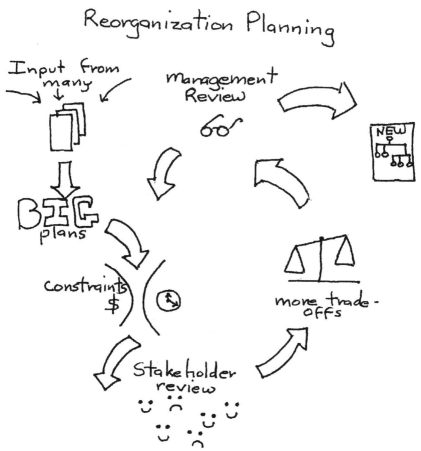

Figure 2.1 Example of a Rich Picture from a RAP

Mapping

Mapping is the use of simple graphics, including drawings, pictures, and sketches. Mapping can be used for collecting data, presenting data, understanding data, and planning action. As a data collection technique, maps are drawn by local participants and the RAP team and can be used to illustrate important information about individuals, social groups, and the wider environment. Spatial mapping includes geographic and social composition of a community, building, or place. Spatial maps can include areas of activity, boundaries, key people, behaviors associated with location, and contextual factors such as income levels or ethnic groups. Spatial maps are only one kind of map, and mapping can be applied to almost anything. Other types of maps include network maps showing relationships between different people and groups, body maps showing the perceived effects of substance use on an individual's health, and information maps showing the distribution of health or social conditions over time.

Mapping can quickly collect and present complex information in a simpler form. Other advantages of mapping are that it can be conducted with people regardless of age, literacy, or familiarity with social science research. Mapping can facilitate shared understanding between the RAP team and the community and it can identify areas in the community where interventions could be located. Mapping may provide for the participation of individuals who would not be comfortable speaking. Maps can identify relationships that otherwise might not be noticed. Figure 2.2 is from a Rapid Appraisal of the health system of the Guarani Indians in Bolivia and maps the relationships between actors and knowledge systems. Participants first identified relevant actors in the health system and then were asked to map the relationship of the actors with sectors and to group actors with good contacts with each other (Umans 1997, 12). (See Team Observing, p. 27.)

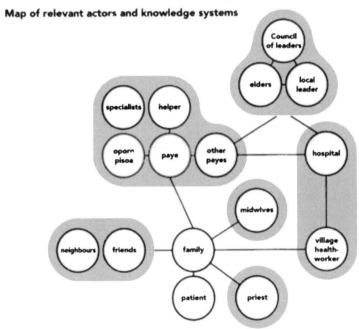

Source: Umans (1997, 12).

Figure 2.2 Map of Relevant Actors and Knowledge Systems (Guarani Indian health system, Bolivia)

Field Notes and Logs

Entire books have been written on **field notes** and there is very little agreement on what constitutes field notes and what you do with them once they have been collected. What is outlined here has worked for some of the teams on which I have participated, but always with some modifications to fit the specific situation. Because more than one person is involved in collecting and processing field notes for a RAP, it is extremely important that all parties agree on the format at the beginning.

Following the suggestion of Ely et al. (1991, 69), I believe the term field notes should be reserved for the usually handwritten notes that are done as the data is being collected. The transcripts of interviews that were recorded can be called field notes or transcripts. The term **log** is reserved for the repository of information from the field notes in a format ready for analysis. Obvious, but sometimes overlooked, is the need to ensure that day of the week, date, time, location, and the name of the individual taking the notes are recorded as part of the field notes. The assumption has to be that loose pages will at some point be separated and thus all pages should be numbered.

Field notes do not have to be neat or even readable by anyone other than the person who takes them. They *must* however be written in a way that clearly indicates the difference between observations and reflections on the observations. Observations include what is heard, for example during an interview, and what is seen. Field notes based on careful, detailed observations as opposed to vague summaries can often help the observer avoid imputing false meaning to people's actions. Pelto and Pelto provide hypothetical field note entries that illustrate the difference between vague notes and notes that preserve the details:

Vague notes:

- A showed hostility toward B.

Concrete notes:

- A scowled and spoke harshly to B, saying a number of negative things, including, "Get the hell out of here Mr. B." He then shook his fist in B's face and walked out of the room. (1978, 70)

I have found it useful to take notes on interviews even when I have been responsible for leading the interview. Note taking forces pauses in the process and can keep it from being rushed. Metzler suggests controlling the interview to accommodate note taking. Answers to questions can be repeated and you can ask if you have heard them correctly. If you have, the next statement can be something like "Okay, let me get this into my notes before we go on" (Metzler 1997, 116). Often, I have also used these pauses to consider where the interview was going and what should come next.

Even when interviews are recorded, there is a need for notes. The most common objection to taking notes during an interview is that it is too difficult for the interviewer to think about guiding the conversation and at the same time have to worry about taking notes. The use of a team during the RAP prevents note taking by the interviewer from being a problem, since someone other than the person leading the discussion can take the notes. Since all team members are expected to participate in the interview process, this can become complicated, and at times it will be useful to have several team members taking notes on different parts of the interview. Notes during a recorded interview serve two important purposes. First, they are needed for recording observations that are not audible. These might include a description of the settings, who else was present (or close enough to hear), the overall demeanor of the respondent, and nonverbal communications like a smile, a yawn, or the tapping of a finger on the desk. A second use of the field notes during a recorded interview is to ensure that important words are not missed because the recorder does not pick them up or that the entire interview is not missed because of a general failure of the tape recorder.

In addition to the observation, the field notes (and the log), will include reflections. These may be referred to as "observer comments," "analytic memos," or "researcher memos." They may include comments about whether a specific research technique was appropriate. These are conversations with oneself about what has occurred, what has been learned, insights, and leads for future action (Ely et al. 1991, 80). Reflections, defined as any comments that are not observations, can be called **MEMOS**. I am spelling MEMOS with all uppercase letters to remind you of the importance of clearly identifying them in both the field notes and the log as your reflections, and not confusing them with observations (things heard or observed). MEMOS are sometimes recorded on the same tape as an interview immediately following the interview. MEMOS can be clearly identified, in both field notes and the log, by including them in brackets (or underlining them) and starting each with the word MEMO. A log might include MEMOS written at the time that the log was prepared and MEMOS added to the log at a later date. Each time a member of the RAP team adds a MEMO to the log, she should identify herself and give the date. For field notes, it is not possible to overemphasize the need to separate observations from reflections, noted in MEMOS.

The log is the data upon which the analysis is conducted. The log is based on the field notes and is usually prepared at a location away from where the observations were collected. Missing words in field notes for interviews that were not recorded are filled in when preparing the log. The log will include the transcripts of recorded interviews. Just as in the field notes, it is critical to distinguish between what was seen and heard and reflections on the observations. Reflections should be clearly identified as MEMOS. MEMOS should be dated and for a RAP their author should be identified. Logs are a chronological record of what the team members learn and their insights.

Anything in the field notes or the log that is not a direct observation should be identified as a MEMO, enclosed with brackets, and dated, and its author should be identified.

Logs are usually most useful if typed, double-spaced, with very wide margins on both sides. Lines may be numbered. In the next chapter we will discuss adding codes, using words and not numbers, to the left margins and margin notes to the right margin (see Coding and Margin Remarks, p. 66). The marginal remarks identify issues that a specific code may be missing or blurring and may suggest revisions to the coding scheme (Miles and Huberman 1994, 67). Figure 3.2, in the next chapter, is an example of a log that includes a MEMO transferred from the field notes, codes, and marginal remarks.

Logs should be prepared within twenty-four hours of the experience. This may be equally important for the lone researcher and the RAP team, since forgetting begins as soon as the experience ends. The completion of the log as soon as possible is absolutely critical for the RAP team, since it is the basis for iterative analysis and additional data collection (see The Twenty-Four-Hour Rule, p. 123). There are no hard-and-fast rules for RAP, but if there were, the completion of logs before moving on to the next data collection cycle would be one of them. Logs should contain as much detail as possible.

> **THE TWENTY-FOUR-HOUR RULE:** Logs should be prepared within twenty-four hours of the interview.

More than twenty techniques associated with ethnography and RAP have been introduced in this chapter. If you are new to qualitative research and ethnography, it may seem a bit overwhelming. To begin experimenting with RAP, all you need to remember is that your goal is to talk with people and get them to tell their stories, as opposed to answering your questions. The different techniques introduced in this chapter can be thought of as tools that can help you better do this. If you at least know a tool exists, you will be able to find it when you need it.

The theme of this chapter has been that two sets of eyes and ears are better than one. The techniques suggested should help make the best use of the extra eyes and ears as part of intensive teamwork. The theme of the next chapter is that two heads are better than one in figuring out what has been seen and heard and what should be seen and heard next before trying once again to make sense out of the data collected. The intensive teamwork implementing the iterative process of data analysis and data collection should help make the best use of the additional heads.

Additional Readings

Three entries from the Essential RAPper Library, p. xxi, are also included here. Bernard (1995) provides in-depth explanations of specific techniques. Creswell (1998) provides an introduction to different aspects of ethnography, includes examples, and identifies key references. Creswell's analytical table of contents by traditions is especially useful. Marshall and

Rossman's (1999) book is especially relevant to ethnography. Schensul and LeCompte's (1999) series of seven books covers the multiple, complex steps of doing ethnographic research. The discussion of research teams and partnerships in volume 6 is especially relevant to RAP. The books by Fetterman (1998) and Hammersley and Atkinson (1995) focus specifically on ethnography and are often cited. Fetterman maintains an excellent web site on *Ethnography and the Internet* that lists databases, free and commercial software, and practical reference pages: <http://www.stanford.edu/~davidf/ethnography.html>. Morgan (1997) is the authority on focus group research.

Bernard, H. R. 1995. *Research methods in anthropology: Qualitative and quantitative approaches.* 2d ed. Walnut Creek, Calif.: AltaMira Press.

Creswell, J. W. 1998. *Qualitative inquiry and research design: Choosing among five traditions.* Thousand Oaks, Calif.: Sage.

Fetterman, D. M. 1998. *Ethnography: Step by step.* 2d ed. Thousand Oaks, Calif.: Sage.

Hammersley, M., and P. Atkinson. 1995. *Ethnography: Principles in practice.* 2d ed. New York: Routledge.

Marshall, C., and B. Rossman. 1999. *Designing Qualitative Research.* 3d ed. Thousand Oaks, Calif.: Sage.

Morgan, D. L. 1997. *Focus groups as qualitative research.* 2d ed. Thousand Oaks, Calif.: Sage.

Schensul, J. J., and M. D. LeCompte. 1999. *Ethnographer's toolkit.* 7 vols. Walnut Creek, Calif.: AltaMira.

ITERATIVE ANALYSIS AND ADDITIONAL DATA COLLECTION

Main Points

1. An iterative process is defined as a process in which replications of a cycle produce results that approximate the desired result more and more closely.
2. The constant shifting between data analysis and additional data collection is an iterative or recursive process.
3. RAP is divided between scheduled blocks of time used for collecting information and blocks of time during which the team engages in data analysis and considers the next round of data collection.
4. The iterative nature of RAP allows for the discovery of the unexpected.
5. The importance of the intensive team interaction before each new cycle of data collection cannot be overemphasized.
6. Before the conclusions are final, the RAP team needs to share them with the people who have provided the information.
7. The joint preparation of the RAP report continues the intensive team interaction.
8. Miles and Huberman's (1994) model of analysis involves three steps: (1) coding the data, (2) displaying it, and (3) drawing conclusions.
9. The critical first step in the analysis process is dividing the log into thought units and applying codes to these units.
10. There are numerous tactics for generating meaning, including (1) identifying patterns and themes, (2) seeing plausibility, (3) clustering, (4) metaphor making, (5) counting, and (6) making contracts and comparisons.

Iteration

An Example

Beginning with the initial meeting with all of the directors of state farms in the Koshlyn region of Poland, the team heard shrill complaints about the high interest rates on loans. Initially, the RAP team focused on this as one of the new uncertainties that state farm directors faced. During one of the evening reviews the decision was made to ask about the manager's understanding of the relationship between interest rates and inflation the next time a manager complained about high interest rates. This produced a vague explanation from the next manager interviewed about the real costs of borrowed money. This issue was placed on a back burner. A visit to a farm where tractors were lined up in the parking lot and crops were beyond ready for harvesting led to a discussion of why the tractors were not in the fields harvesting the crops. The director of the farm indicated credit was not available to purchase fuel for the tractors because the "high interest rates" on a previous loan had made it impossible to repay. Team discussion on these results led to the decision to initiate a new line of questions with the next director on the traditional sources of cash needed for different operations. This led to an explanation of the old system, where state farms had easy access to very cheap loans from the state bank. These loans, however, were tools the Communist Party and the state used to limit the initiative and behavior of the state farms. For example, an initiative by a state farm to expand into a new crop, a new process activity, or even a new enterprise, like tourism, required a loan, and with the loan came close state control. Cash-flow management and timing of events to produce funds needed for the next activity had not been an issue with the old system and the less successful managers had failed to recognize the change in the system. The RAP team pursued this with the next director and discovered similar descriptions. The need for improvements in cash-flow management became one of the least-expected but most important findings of the RAP team.

Iteration and Ethnography

The example above illustrates the iterative process of beginning to tease out the essential meaning, then using this initial analysis to guide additional data collection, and then repeating the process. The almost constant shifting between data analysis and additional data collection is an iterative, or recursive, process. An iterative process is a process in which replications of a cycle produce results that approximate the desired result more and more closely. Each cycle of data analysis and data collection is expected to produce better and better results. This same process is labeled by some social scientists as a recursive process. A recursive process is a process that can repeat itself indefinitely or until a specified condition is met. One of the specific conditions that should be met during ethnographic research is for the data to begin to repeat themselves. When this occurs, the additional data will not have a significant impact on the analysis. The goal of the analysis process is to draw conclusions from the data that can be shared with others in an economical and interesting fashion.

Iteration and RAP

The RAP team, like the ethnographer, often begins with information collected in advance and then progressively learns from information provided by semistructured interviews and direct observations. For the RAP team, the data collection process, with its focus on triangulation, is enhanced by intensive team interaction. The RAP team, again like the ethnographer, engages in a similar process of iterative data analysis and collection of additional information. For the RAP team, a strict schedule that from the very beginning of the process divides time between analysis and additional data collection facilitates intensive team interaction.

> **RAP is divided between time for collecting information and time for analysis of information.**

RAP is divided between scheduled blocks of time used for collecting information and blocks of time during which the team engages in data analysis and considers the next round of data collection. Even as the team reviews the data collected so far and begins to consider possible conclusions, the team makes conscious decisions about additional methodology and lines of inquiry. Specific decisions will be made on questions to revise, add, or delete; methods and techniques to change; and locations and individuals who need to be visited.

Intensive team interaction during this process allows the team to benefit from the perspectives of the different team members. The chances that important issues will be missed decline as input from different team members increases. The discussions on possible conclusions early in the process ensure that even during a short RAP there is time to try out new lines of inquiry in the field and to test possible conclusions against new data.

While the RAP team is searching for trends, patterns, and opportunities for generalization, the iterative nature of the process allows for the discovery of the unexpected. RAP can be thought of as an open system in which what is learned from feedback is used to progressively change the system. The research effort is structured to encourage the RAP team to rapidly change questions, interviews, and direction as new information is gathered. One of the most serious problems with the implementation of RAP is the failure to allow sufficient time for multiple iterations.

Techniques Associated with Iterative Analysis and Additional Data Collection

Structuring the Research Time

Opinions differ considerably on how to structure the time of a RAP, but there is almost universal agreement on the importance of explicitly scheduling time for collecting data and specific time for team meetings to make sense out of the collected data. Regularly scheduled team meetings help build team cohesion and provide opportunities for interaction between the insiders and the outsiders on the team. As noted earlier, the scheduling of time for analysis should start at the beginning of the RAP. Scheduling time for team analysis early in the process is necessary to ensure that there will be adequate time for returning to the field to collect additional information, analyze this new information, and then, based on this analysis, return to the field for even more information.

Beginning on day one, schedule time for team interaction.

Schedules should include blocks of time for analysis before a new cycle of data collection is scheduled to begin. If data collection is a daily process, there is a need for daily blocks of time for analysis. In addition, a longer block of time may be necessary at least once a week to review the overall status of the RAP. These weekly meetings may focus more on the identification of possible conclusions than will the daily meetings, in which the focus may be more on immediate decisions on what additional data to collect and the best strategies for collecting. Sometime in the middle of the process the schedule should include time to prepare for and make presentations to the local people (see below). Large blocks of time will be needed near the end of the RAP to prepare the report and to review the process. The importance of the intensive team interaction before each new cycle of data collection cannot be overemphasized.

While each individual RAP is an iterative process, a RAP can also be part of a larger iterative process in which its results are considered exploratory and subject to change based on a subsequent RAP, other research, or the monitoring and evaluation of an intervention resulting from the RAP. The RAP checklist includes scheduling a review of the results and possibly updating the report.

Checking Back with Informants

> **Share tentative results with local participants before the conclusions are final.**

Before the conclusions are final, the RAP team should share them with the people who have provided the information and check for agreement. This can be done either formally or informally, but the purpose should be made clear to the local people. The local people can provide corrections to facts and their own interpretation of the situation. Preparation for a presentation of results provides the RAP team with the opportunity for intensive interaction concerning emerging conclusions and gaps in the data. Even before the presentation is made, the research agenda can be expected to change. Team presentation of the tentative results allows for a division of labor, with one or two members focusing on the presentation and the other members focusing on the response, both verbal and nonverbal, from the local people. Ideally, team members who are not presenting should be sitting with the local people. Informal comments from the local people at this stage can be especially useful. A part of the presentation should be to ask advice on how the team might focus its remaining time, with attention to who else should be interviewed. In addition to its role as a technique associated with the iterative process, checking back with the local participants is a critical part of the data analysis process. The role in data analysis of checking back with the local participants is discussed in the section on Techniques for Data Analysis, below.

RAP Report Preparation by the Team

The joint preparation of the RAP report continues the intensive team interaction started with preparations for reporting back to the local people. The preparation of the report should start while there is still time for additional data collection. Presentation by team members to each other accelerates the analysis process and allows input on possible conclusions from different disciplinary perspectives. Gaps in information that may not be apparent to one team member are unlikely to escape detection by the entire team. The involvement of the entire team, including the local members, in the report preparation provides the report with a level of cross-checking that is impossible with reports prepared by a single individual.

The entire RAP team should write the RAP report.

The RAP report should be written using a vocabulary and style that is most readable to the intended audience with the lowest level of formal education. The team is cautioned to avoid "Greek-fed, polysyllabic bull-shit" (Booth 1979 as cited in Becker 1986, 10). Becker (1986) provides excellent advice on overcoming writer's block, writing and revising (again and again), and adopting a persona compatible with lucid prose.

Sometimes a RAP report can have greater impact if it is not the traditional, narrative report. Sobrevila, an ecologist with the Nature Conservancy, directed a Rapid Ecological Assessment team whose end product was color-coded maps of an area's vegetative cover. A team of local and Nature Conservancy biologists spent two to three weeks exploring an area and identifying flora and fauna. All of this information was compiled in maps showing different classes of vegetation and estimating the wildlife potential. Sobrevila states, "We believe maps are a strong conservation tool" (Abate 1992, 486).

Data Analysis

There are numerous ways of analyzing ethnographic data. There is no one best way and ethnographers often are informal in their approach to analysis. Miles and Huberman's (1994) comments about the research process appear especially relevant to analysis: "To us it seems clear that research is actually more a craft than a slavish adherence to methodological rules. No study conforms exactly to a standard methodology; each one calls for the researcher to bend the methodology to the peculiarities of the setting" (4).

> **There is no one best way for analyzing qualitative data.**

An approach to analysis that has worked for me is based on Miles and Huberman's (1994) model. This model of analysis involves three steps: (1) coding the data and adding marginal remarks, (2) displaying it, and (3) drawing conclusions. Figure 3.1 illustrates the relationship of these aspects of analysis and the relationships of the analysis to data collection.

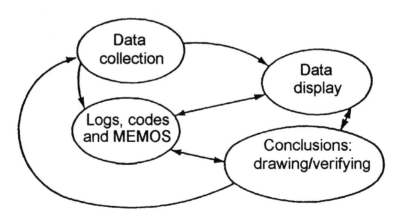

Source: Miles and Huberman (1994), fig 1.4.

Figure 3.1. Components of Data Analysis: Interactive Model

Other ethnographers (see Wolcott 1994) use different categories and a different vocabulary to describe a similar process. For ethnographic research, data analysis is an ongoing process that can begin before any data is collected (for example when the guidelines are being prepared) and continues through the preparation of the final report.

> Start the data analysis process before you end data collection.

Techniques for Data Analysis

Coding and Margin Remarks

The logs are the source of the data for making sense out of a situation (see the section on Field Notes and Logs, p. 54). The first step in the analysis process is to read the logs. Logs are read, reread, and reread again. Several authors recommend that logs be read a minimum of three times before anything else is done. Logs need to be reread again before additional data is collected, during the data analysis process, and while the report is being prepared. The next step in the analysis process is dividing the log into thought units and applying codes to these units. A unit of thought may be a sentence, paragraph, several paragraphs, or even an individual word. **Coding** is the key to the process of selecting, focusing, simplifying, abstracting, and transforming the data that appears in the logs. Coding, like data display and conclusion drawing, occurs continuously throughout the research. It may even start before any data has been collected, when decisions are made on research questions, specific research techniques, whom to interview, and conceptual frameworks (Miles and Huberman 1994, 10). Coding is often the most time-consuming aspect of the data analysis process.

Coding can be thought of as cutting the logs into strips and placing the strips into piles. The codes are the labels you give the individual piles. Some researchers physically cut the logs into strips or use qualitative computer analysis software such as NUD*IST to divide the log into units to which codes can be applied. In many cases and for many researchers, writing codes in the margins of the logs is sufficient for analysis. I have found writing codes in the margins of the logs adequate for RAPs.

Developing a coding system is based on trial and error and more trial and error. It is critical that the coding system remains flexible. The persons assigning codes are looking for threads that tie together bits of data. They are looking for recurring words or phrases. These words often become the labels for the codes. Many experienced researchers suggest having only five or six major codes and, where necessary, dividing these codes into subcodes. Coding can be thought of as winnowing, since not all information may be relevant or have to be coded. You can always return to the log and code material that was not coded and change the coding done earlier. It should be noted that a single unit of thought will often have multiple codes.

> **Start with only five or six codes. Subdivide these when necessary.**

Entire chapters and major sections of articles have been written on coding, with each suggesting a somewhat different approach (Bogdan and Biklen 1992; Giorgi 1989; Goetz and LeCompte 1984; Lofland and Lofland 1984; Miles and Huberman 1984; Strauss and Corbin 1990; Tesch 1990; Wolcott 1994). Marshall and Rossman's (1999) chapter on "Recording, Managing, and Analyzing Data" provides a succinct introduction to these topics that will be especially useful for the less-experienced researcher. I have found that the best way of learning to code logs is practicing the process in small groups of two or three people.

> **Time spent coding logs can help prevent jumping to premature conclusions.**

Adding **margin remarks** is closely related to the coding process. Margin remarks are usually written into the margin of the log after it has been typed. Almost anything can be included in a margin remark, but often they are related to the coding activity. Margin remarks made during the coding process include ideas and reactions to the meaning of statements that may not be consistent with codes. Sometimes, margin remarks suggest new interpretations and connections with other parts of the data. Margin remarks can identify themes involving several different codes. Sometimes, trying to differentiate between codes and themes can be a waste of time. Margin remarks may identify issues for the next wave of data collection. Some authors suggest that codes be placed in the left margin of the log and that margin notes be placed in the right margin. Regardless of which side of the log is reserved for codes, everyone who will use the log needs to agree. Margin remarks often include comments similar to some of the comments in MEMOS, with the major difference being that MEMOS are usually typed and margin remarks are usually handwritten and added after the log has been prepared. Figure 3.2 is an example of a log based on several different interviews conducted at different times and includes a MEMO, codes, and marginal notes.

Data Display

The second aspect of analysis is **data display**. Being the second aspect of the analysis process should not be confused with being the second step. There is no particular order in which the data-display and conclusion-drawing aspects of data analysis should occur, and even coding is likely to continue throughout the analysis process. Miles and Huberman (1994, 10) define a display as "an organized, compressed assembly of information that permits conclusion drawing and action." They argue that the extended amounts of text found in logs can be very difficult to use for drawing conclusions, since they are dispersed, sequential, poorly structured, and bulky. They argue for better displays of data, including different types of matrices, graphs, charts, and networks. Data displays that compare different cases can be especially useful. The data display should assemble organized information into an accessible, compact form. This allows the analyst to "see what is happening" and either draw conclusions or move on to the next step in the analysis (11). As with data reduction, the creation and use of displays is part of analysis. Figure 3.3 illustrates a data display based on one type of matrix. There are numerous other types of matrices, as well as different types of graphs, charts, and networks. A rich picture (see figure 2.1, p. 52) can also be used as a data display.

SS purpose

MG. It is my endeavor here to always serve students and specifically those who need assistance. I can tell you it's not always easy to focus on serving students when you're in the hot seat that we are usually in. We do remind ourselves over and repeatedly -- that is what we are dong here and that is what we are about. It's rewarding and the students are enjoyable. I have worked a very long time; we are forever changing. We have new things thrown at us every year.

enjoy S

regulations

enjoy S

tech.

S not prep.

KK. I like students. That is why I am here. I've always been in education with regards to hanging around students, and I like that. I don't like touch-tone. I think it is impersonal, cold and half of the time the students don't read the instruction. The students have to come back and see me anyway because they couldn't get registered.

leadership

↓ resources

AR. (1) It's been a battle in the last seven years because of a particular administrator. . .who didn't really value what we were doing as we would have liked and wanted to do away with position and do a lot more curriculum advisors. The results was that over those year we lot a lot of position due to attrition. This was due to retirement or people taking jobs in other areas. Those positions were not refilled.

downsize be
attrition /problem
of fairness

tech.

AR. (2) Some things came up, after I talked with you and talked with the counselors, that I wanted to bring to your attention. One of the big problems that we're having right now is technology. Our technology is trying to match up registration with the Web and with touch-tone and is being hampered because of prerequisite codes.

tech. problem
due to ↓
resources

↓ resources

There is a push in the whole wide world to go technology. And yet, there is the reality that people are really dragging their feet. . . .We want to help students.
- - -

overwork

Right now, it's just creating a massive amount of work for us that we shouldn't have to be doing.
- - -

unfair distribution
of work

[MEMO December 3, JB. This was AR's second interview. He was insistent that he needed more time with the team. He clearly had an agenda of items he wanted to cover.]

S= Students
SS= Student Services

Figure 3.2. RAP Log Illustrating Memos, Codes, and Marginal Remarks

Conclusion Drawing and Verification

The third element (but not necessarily the third step) of analysis is conclusion drawing and verification. "From the start of data collection, the qualitative analyst is beginning to decide what things mean—is noting regularities, patterns, explanations, possible configuration, causal flows, and propositions" (Miles and Huberman 1994, 11). Miles and Huberman suggest that people can make sense of the most chaotic events, but that the critical question is whether the meanings they find in qualitative data

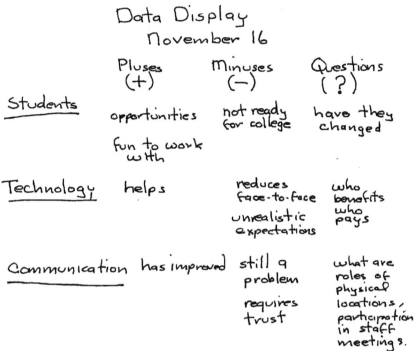

Data Display
November 16

Pluses (+)	Minuses (−)	Questions (?)
Students		
opportunities	not ready for college	have they changed
fun to work with		
Technology	helps	reduces face-to-face	who benefits
		unrealistic expectations	who pays
Communication	has improved	still a problem	what are roles of physical locations, participation in staff meetings.
		requires trust	

Figure 3.3. Example of a Data Display

are "valid, repeatable, and right" (245). They identify and explain thirteen tactics for generating meaning. The first six of these are more descriptive than the others, provide a good beginning point for most research, and will be briefly introduced here. The first three focus on helping to identify "what goes with what" and are concerned with (1) patterns and themes, (2) seeing plausibility, and (3) clustering. The next three tactics for generating meaning, (4) metaphor making, (5) counting, and (6) making contrasts and comparisons, are less concrete, more conceptual, and focus on sharpening understandings.

1. *Noting patterns, themes.* Patterns pull together separate pieces of data. Among other things, patterns can be based on similarities and differences or connections in time and space. Miles and Huberman suggest that patterns occur so quickly and easily that there is no need for how-to advice: "Something 'jumps out' at you, [and] suddenly makes sense." They caution that

sometimes patterns happen too quickly and note that "beliefs in the existence of patterns are remarkably resistant to new evidence" (246).

2. *Seeing plausibility.* Sometimes conclusions are plausible, make good sense, or fit and are based on intuition more than anything else: "It just feels right" (246). Miles and Huberman recommend, "Trust your 'plausibility' intuitions, but don't fall in love with them" (247).

3. *Clustering* consists of "clumping things into classes, categories, bins" (248) and involves putting together things that are like each other. Examples of behavior might be clustered together as "controlling," "directive," or "neglectful." Categories often require other categories to define them, as when the category "automobile" is based on the categories of "wheel" and "engine" (248). Clusters may overlap and need not be mutually exclusive. Miles and Huberman (249) note it can be more difficult to cluster complex things that have many attributes that may be relevant to the clustering task. They suggest using a "case-by-attribute matrix," in which cases are listed as rows and attributes are listed as columns. The contents of the columns will suggest which attributes are critical for clustering the cases. Once again, they suggest that conclusions based on clustering be held lightly to prevent premature closure (250).

4. *Metaphor making* is suggested as a way of integrating diverse pieces of data. **Metaphors** involve comparing two things based on their similarities while ignoring their differences. Miles and Huberman note that people, including the people we study, constantly use metaphors as a way of making sense of their experience. Miles and Huberman (1994, 250) suggest that there is a need to be aware of the metaphors used by both the researcher and the people studied and that the researcher should "dig into them for implicit meanings, for more explicit exploration and testing" (250). They suggest asking questions like "What does it feel like?" and "If I only had two words to describe an important feature at this site, what would they be?" as a way of generating

metaphors. Follow-up to the reference to "my private prison" by one of the participants in the community college RAP led to a discussion of physical office space, the participant's perception that she was being observed, and her relationship with her supervisor. Miles and Huberman caution about looking for overarching metaphors too early in a study, since doing so can distract you from fieldwork and lead to hasty judgments. They also recommend knowing "when to stop pressing the metaphor for its juice" (252).

5. *Counting* is suggested as a familiar way of seeing what is there. Miles and Huberman identify three reasons for using numbers as part of the process for generating meanings. Numbers help the researcher to see rapidly a large amount of data, to verify a hunch or hypothesis, and to stay honest. Miles and Huberman caution that numbers should not be ignored (253).

6. *Making contrasts/comparisons* is identified as a time-honored way to test a conclusion by drawing a contrast or making a comparison between two sets of things. Comparisons are based on asking the question, "How does X differ from Y?" The focus is on the contrast between sets of things, such as persons, roles, activities, and cases, that we know to differ in some important respect.

The process that has been outlined for analyzing the results of a RAP has included (1) data coding and the related activity of preparing margin remarks; (2) data display, with emphasis on graphical ways of organizing information; and (3) conclusion drawing, with emphasis on six specific tactics for generating meaning. An important aspect of conclusion drawing is verification. According to Miles and Huberman:

> Verification may be as brief as a fleeting second thought crossing the analyst's mind during writing, with a short excursion back to the field notes, or it may be thorough and elaborate, with lengthy argumentation and review among colleagues to develop "intersubjective consensus," or with extensive efforts to replicate a finding in another data set. (1994, 11)

Without verification, they argue "we are left with interesting stories about what happened, of unknown truth and utility" (11).

How Much Data Is Needed?

Every ethnographer faces the question of how much data is needed and how much time in the field and what number of interviews are sufficient. The data are sufficient when they begin repeating themselves (Ely et al. 1991, 158). The criterion of redundancy states that when data repeat themselves, it is time to stop. Ely et al. suggest, "It is far easier but perhaps more unsettling to know when enough is *not* enough" (159).

When themes begin to repeat, it is time to stop.

Checking Back with Informants

Checking back with the informants for the RAP is an important aspect of the data analysis process as well as a part of the iterative process of data analysis and additional data collection. A study can be considered trustworthy when the people who provide the information are willing to agree with the analysis of the researcher. Checking back with the local participants lets the RAP team know if participants agree and allows the team to collect additional information and revisit the analysis process if there is disagreement. Checking back with the local Ministry of Agriculture officials during the Polish state farms RAP was critical for the identification of specific issues that could be addressed at the local level. The officials confirmed that some directors of state farms were using the rhetoric of a market economy but did not really understand the meaning. This became a specific area where the local Ministry of Agriculture could provide support for these directors. The local officials also confirmed the observation that some directors did not recognize that other directors were relatively more successful and that lessons could be learned from them. This became a second area of intervention for the local Ministry of Agriculture. Checking back with the participants in the community college RAP confirmed the identification of specific areas that needed change and allowed the participants to begin to address some of these issues without waiting for the report. Checking your interpretation periodically with the people who are being studied is sometimes referred to as "**member checking**" (Lincoln and Guba 1985).

The next chapter explores the issue of teamwork as an element of RAP, with careful attention to the experience of the Polish State Farm RAP. While teamwork is not new to ethnographic research, it is not the norm. A bit of background on the use of teamwork should therefore be helpful in understanding the issues faced by the RAP team. Some of the examples discussed in the next chapter will not be completely consistent with the methodology discussed in the preceding chapters. This should not come as a surprise or be a cause for concern. Flexibility and the adaptation to local conditions and resources available are defining characteristics of RAP.

Additional Readings

Miles and Huberman (1994) provide the best model I know of for data analysis and detailed instructions and examples. Ely et al. (1991) and Marshall and Rossman (1999) have chapters that provide more general approaches to analysis. Becker (1986) provides excellent advice on writing, with specific attention to editing to achieve readable prose.

Becker, H. S. 1986. *Writing for social scientists*. Chicago: University of Chicago Press.

Ely, M., M. Anzul, T. Friedman, D. Garner, and A. M. Steinmetz. 1991. *Doing qualitative research: Circles within circles*. Bristol, Pa.: Falmer Press.

Marshall, C., and B. Rossman. 1999. *Designing qualitative research*. 3d ed. Thousand Oaks, Calif.: Sage.

Miles, M. B., and A. M. Huberman. 1994. *Qualitative data analysis: An expanded sourcebook*. 2d ed. Thousand Oaks, Calif.: Sage.

CHAPTER FOUR

TEAMWORK: POLISH STATE FARMS AND THE COMMUNITY COLLEGE

Main Points

1. RAP is premised on teamwork and the success of RAP depends upon the quality of the teamwork.
2. The assumption is that the RAP team will be together most of the time and will work together in data collection and analysis, including the preparation of the report.
3. For teamwork to increase productivity, team members must bring to the team different perspectives and expertise.
4. Several sets of eyes and ears and constant team interaction are essential for getting the most from the very short time in the field.
5. In both cases discussed in the chapter, by the end of the field-work, the teams were spending as much or more time talking with each other and trying to make sense out of what was being observed as they were on observing new things.
6. The ability of RAP to begin the process of achieving an emic understanding of a situation in a short time requires the use of a team of researchers, with at least one team member an insider.
7. Even when the rest of the RAP team has gone on to other things, the insiders continue to be called upon to clarify results, resolve pending issues, and help organize local responses to the results.
8. Teamwork to some extent depends upon team leadership.
9. The five most critical responsibilities of the team leader are (1) providing orientation, (2) keeping activity focused and responsive to changing conditions, (3) maintaining morale, (4) team building, and (5) ensuring that administrative support is provided.

Introduction to the RAPs which Provide the Examples of Teamwork

RAP is premised on teamwork, and the success of RAP depends upon the quality of the teamwork. As explained in the preceding chapters, team interaction is critical for both the data collection and data analysis processes. Team interaction depends upon the mix of people on the team and each member understanding her or his responsibility. RAP teams usually include one or more insiders as well as the outsiders. The role of insiders is extremely important and will be given special attention. Finally, the role of leadership in facilitating teamwork deserves close attention. I will draw on the RAPs of the Polish state farms and a community college to illustrate teamwork. Even though the original documentation on the Polish state farms used the label "Rapid Appraisal," the process meets the requirements of RAP and that term is used here. The examples are meant to suggest some of the many ways that teamwork can be implemented and are not intended to provide models for implementing RAP. Because of the extensive use of examples from these RAPs, a brief introduction for each will be useful.

The Example of the Polish State Farms RAP

In 1989 the government of Poland, at the end of more than forty years of Communist rule, announced that state industries would be privatized. Inflation accelerated rapidly in 1989 and the economy faltered. On January 1, 1990, the government instituted what was called the "big bang" by decontrolling prices, slashing subsidies, and drastically reducing import barriers. The transition to a market economy proved especially difficult in the agricultural sector. The Communists had consolidated most of the small private farms into collectives, but "state farms," owned and directly managed by the state, controlled 25 percent of the agricultural production. State farms were large enterprises often consisting of several different sites and multiple enterprises including crops, livestock, and processing. They were generally responsible for providing housing and social services like schools and medical care to their workers. Despite the 1989 announcement, none of the state farms had been privatized by mid-1991 and there was growing concern in Poland that many of these farms would fail and their resources would be lost. The government of Poland approached the

U.S. Department of Agriculture (USDA) for assistance on this issue. The four American team members arrived in Poland in early September 1991, less than ten weeks after the USDA requested that I organize and lead a RAP. The American members of the team joined the Polish team member in Warsaw. The entire team spent three days in Warsaw, sixteen in the province of Koszalin, and four back in Warsaw working on the report and briefing Polish Ministry of Agriculture officials. The English version of the final report was finished seventeen days later and the Polish version twenty-four days after the English version. The team traveled more than twenty-five hundred kilometers in Koszalin during the course of the RAP. Team members observed livestock production facilities, fields under regular cultivation, experimental fields, processing plants, apartments, two private farms, and a cooperative store run by a group of private farmers. The team conducted extensive semistructured interviews, averaging more than four hours each with the directors of ten carefully selected state farms. In addition to the ten directors, the team interviewed a livestock unit manager, the chairman of a workers council, the director of a state farm not visited, and a combine tractor driver. Team members participated in meetings with all of the directors of state farms in the region, the mayors of four municipalities, bank officials, researchers from the potato research center in Koszalin, and the director of an agricultural secondary school. More than 110 hours of interviews produced 110 pages of typed field notes.

The purpose of this RAP was to assess management responses to the economic environment with the objective of identifying what, if any, interventions might stabilize the farms until they could be privatized. The team found that the responses of state farm directors to the changes in the economy ranged from no response to changes in organizational structure, crop and livestock production, financial management, levels of employment, and marketing. These responses were analyzed based on the directors' explanations of what had happened. The responses suggested that many state farm directors did not fully understand how a market operates. This lack of full understanding was most serious in areas of (1) risk, (2) information, (3) production versus profits, (4) price determination, and (5) financial (cash-flow) management.

The RAP team identified a role for the Polish Ministry of Agriculture to play in helping the managers of the state farms better deal with the changing economy of Poland. The primary thrust of this assistance was helping directors and others address the issues of risk, information, profits, price determination, and financial management. Specific programs were proposed for (1) helping them locate and interpret market information necessary to predict a range of likely prices, (2) helping them adjust production decisions in response to this range of prices, and (3) helping them improve financial management, beginning with cash-flow analysis, in order to implement decisions based on price estimates. The executive summary for the report is in appendix B.

The Example of the Community College RAP

As noted in chapter 1, the RAP at a community college in the Pacific Northwest was initiated by the newly hired dean of the Student Services Division. She understood enough of the depth of mistrust among the employees in her division and the complexity of the issues related to it to know that something other than a traditional approach to understanding was needed. She was aware that not enough was known about these issues to formulate questions that could be used for questionnaire-based research and that there was insufficient time to do traditional qualitative research. She asked me to organize a RAP focusing on the organizational structure of her division.

Most of the employees in the Student Services Division first learned that there would be a RAP from an e-mail message. While the message outlined the essential elements of the methodology, it did not address the issue of the objectives for the RAP. It also failed to provide information on who would be participating in the study or the proposed time line. On the first day, the RAP team met with the leadership group from the division. At that point, questions were raised about the objectives of the study, how the RAP team had been chosen, how much control the college had over the RAP team composition, how much the study was costing, who would "own" the results, and how the data would be used. The team provided straightforward answers to these questions. There was a series of questions about confidentiality and it was stated that some individuals would find it very difficult to participate since they had been harmed in the past by being "open." A joke about the room being bugged elicited a serious discussion about an instance when a past administrator had in fact listened in on a meeting of the administrator's subordinates. The level of suspicion is illustrated by the concern of two participants who did not want anyone concerned with the college to be involved in transcribing their interviews. There was real concern about how choices would be made on who would be interviewed and whether all units and positions would be included. There was some concern about the qualitative process of identifying themes from the information collected. The RAP team asked the leadership group to inform the individuals in their units about the RAP and to suggest individuals who might begin the process.

The RAP did not begin with a preset list of people to be interviewed. Most participants were self-identified or were identified by their colleagues as individuals who should be included. Once a few individuals had been interviewed, there was a flood of individuals who wanted to be interviewed.

The team briefed an expanded version of the leadership group about three-fourths of the way through the process and received feedback on the tentative themes that had been identified. By this point a growing number of individuals still wanted to be interviewed. The RAP team made a decision to name an arbitrary end point for interviews and to encourage individuals who still wanted to contribute to put their thoughts in writing and to submit them to the team. Individuals interviewed included fourteen people from the Student Services Division, one senior administrator from outside of this division, and three students. Almost all interviews were recorded and transcribed. By the time the last interviews were conducted, it was clear that there were major differences in opinions. As noted in chapter 1, one of the significant results of the RAP was the identification of the differences in how "students" and "services" were defined by the participants. Six constraints were identified that participants felt prevented them from doing as good a job as they would like to. They involved: (1) communication; (2) physical space; (3) technology; (4) utilization of people's time, talents, and creativity; (5) increases in the number and complexity of regulations; and (6) inadequate resources. After the report was completed, the RAP team was invited back to make a general presentation to almost everyone in the division. Even before the RAP was finished, the leadership of the community college started to address some of the issues that were identified. After the final report was submitted, teams were organized and funding was made available to tackle specific problem areas. Additional information about the findings of the community college RAP can be found in appendix A.

The Tradition of Teamwork

Most qualitative research is conducted by lone researchers, even though the tradition of team research extends back to the beginning of ethnographic research. If joint authorship of articles is used as a rough indicator of team research, less than 30 percent of research is performed by teams (Erickson and Stull 1998, 5). Ethnographic research is generally described as an individual undertaking. Van Maanen et al. use the phrase "one man, one tribe"(1998, vi) to describe the tradition, even as they note the phrase is politically incorrect and historically inaccurate.

Erickson and Stull contend that the trend is for increased use of teams in the conduct of qualitative research. They suggest qualitative researchers can expect to be on teams with other qualitative researchers and to represent the field of qualitative research on multidisciplinary teams (Erickson and Stull 1998, 60). They note that there is a greater likelihood that teams will be involved in applied qualitative research than in nonapplied research.

When teams are used to conduct traditional qualitative research, there is often the assumption that team members will be assigned to different sites and be involved in "different arenas of observation" (Erickson and Stull 1998, 18). They refer to a team research effort where team members were rarely together in one place at one time during the two-and-a-half-year study. However, the assumption is that the RAP team will be together most of the time and will work together in data collection and data analysis, including the preparation of the report.

> The RAP team is together most of the time when working on data collection and data analysis.

Erickson and Stull argue, "teams are not necessarily more efficient than lone rangers in getting their work done, but they can be much more productive" (1998, 36). The increased productivity results from individual team members seeing or not seeing various things and having different interpretations for what they do see (10). Erickson and Stull suggest that it may not be necessary for team members to see the same things at the same time. However, they imply there are advantages for having the team together and doing the observation at the same time (18, 38).

There are some disadvantages to a team approach to research. Given that "the cult of individualism is the state religion of academia" (Erickson and Stull 1998, 54), team research may be more difficult to use for promotion and tenure than research done alone. This will not be an issue for practitioners of RAP outside of academia. Team interaction may make the experience frustrating. Potential sources of conflict include differences in personal style, theoretical and methodological disagreements, divided loyalties, competing professional demands, and unclear lines of authority and responsibility (12). The time team members spend interacting with each other may mean less time interacting with the cultural system they are investigating (55). The researcher involved in traditional qualitative research may have a choice of whether to work alone or as part of a team. This is not a choice for the RAP-based research, since only a team can do it.

Teamwork and Data Collection

Putting Together the Multidisciplinary Team

For teamwork to increase productivity, team members have to be able to bring to the team different perspectives and expertise. In organizing the Polish state farms team and the community college team, I attempted to maximize variability on the teams within the constraints imposed by the availability of individuals to serve on the teams. Based on the expressed needs of the USDA, I concluded that the team in Poland would have to have an economist and an agricultural production specialist. As I started the search for individuals who would be available to participate on the team, I became increasingly aware that the team would benefit from an administrative-organizations specialist, especially someone familiar with Polish culture. I suggested to the USDA that the Polish member of the team should have a relevant technical background. They found an agricultural engineer who had experience with state farms.

For the community college RAP, my objective was to recruit a multidisciplinary team whose members were at least familiar with the basic concepts of RAP. All three team members were students in the Doctoral Program in Leadership at Gonzaga University at the time of the study. Two of them had already taken my qualitative methods course. The first team member had a master's degree in engineering, a faculty appointment in the School of Business, and extensive experience in the private sector dealing with information technology and systems analysis. The second team member had a master's degree in nursing, a faculty position in the Nursing Program, and several years experience with program administration and higher education administration in general. The third team member had a master's degree in counseling psychology, had prior experience with student services in higher education at another institution of higher education, and had been employed for four years by the community college where the RAP was done.

Diversity

Erickson and Stull note the importance of ethnic, gender, age, and background differences in teams for traditional qualitative research. They state that this diversity simultaneously intrudes on and enables the team's efforts to "listen and observe carefully" (Erickson and Stull 1998, 35). They note the importance of gender diversity, and claim that without it teams may miss or misinterpret much of their fieldwork (40). Since the RAP team spends less time in the field and has significantly less time to establish rapport, the diversity of the team can be critical in building linkages.

For the Polish state farms study, different individuals on the team interacted with each other with varying levels of comfort. In some cases a shared professional vocabulary was more important than language fluency. Age similarities facilitated communication, especially with individuals who were either particularly young or old. The shared status of being professional women in a male-dominated sector provided a special link between the female member of our team and the woman from the Ministry of Agriculture who was a part-time member of the team. The latter accompanied the team for many of the visits and provided liaison between the team and the ministry. The differences in status that Polish officials ascribed to different team members appeared to facilitate their communication with these individuals.

The community college RAP team members were well known to each other and enjoyed working together. As noted earlier, two of the team members had been introduced to RAP in a qualitative research course taught by the team leader. Familiarity with each other and with the approach facilitated teamwork. One of the team members commented that she was pleased "with how well the RAP team worked together. Each member's skill level was readily apparent. The chemistry of the group was amazing." From the first interviews, there was comfort with team interviewing. All members of the team shared the role of team spokesperson and different members made presentations. The fact that three team members had experience with community colleges facilitated establishing rapport with numerous participants. The community college RAP team was made up of three women and a man, and included an Asian American.

The experiences of the teams in both Poland and the community college suggest that in some cases diversity is critical for enabling a team to proceed rapidly. However, the experience also confirms the observation of Erickson and Stull that the ethnicity of the fieldworkers and the diversity within the team is not always sufficient to guarantee easy access (1998, 43).

Team Dynamics

In contrast to traditional qualitative research, in which team members are often assigned to different sites and involved in different observations, RAP is based on most of the team being together most of the time. The diverse, multidisciplinary team is the major source for triangulation of data. The assumption is that given the differences in backgrounds, different team members will be seeing and hearing different things. When visiting different swine production facilities in Poland, the production specialist on the team noted differences in the feed. This in turn allowed the team to begin exploring the differences in the way farm managers viewed and were using information. Questions about large, above-ground pipes led to an understanding of the relationship between state farms and the workers who lived in apartments on the farms, and for whom the pipes provided heat from a central power source. The economic collapse of farms would literally turn off the heat, with devastating results for workers and retired workers who lived on the farm.

The economist, production specialist, and systems specialist were all bothered by answers from some managers to questions about production that on the surface did not make sense. Answers to follow-up questions and subsequent analysis of these answers provided the beginning point for understanding that some of the managers were confusing production and productivity. For each interview, the team would agree on who would take the lead in asking questions, but everyone was expected to participate in every interview.

A major concern at the community college was problems with technology, including the lack of technical support and inappropriate applications. One of the RAP team members' fluency in computer talk facilitated these conservations. Discussions of the special needs of international students were facilitated by the international student experience of the team leader as a graduate student in the Philippines. The significance of having four or five signs pointing the way to the new office of one of the administrators likely would have been missed by most researchers. The physical presence of a team of researchers in the location and interviewing some individuals in their offices resulted in one member commenting on the number of signs. This led to a discussion of the reasons behind the move of this administrator, which in turn led to a rich discussion on communication problems.

Both teams discussed in advance the need to prevent respondents from feeling that a gang of researchers was attacking them. The use of an interpreter in Poland for much of the questioning helped ensure that there was time between questions and follow-up comments. The presence of Polish speakers on the team helped the interpreters understand questions involving unfamiliar technical terms and helped to ensure that responses were reported in full. The team decided that two or three of its members could do a better job with some visits and interviews. In one case in Poland, after it became obvious that the team approach to questioning was leaving the respondent uncomfortable, the economist completed the interview by himself.

In Poland the team shared the responsibility for taking notes, since interviews were not taped. From the beginning, everyone knew that field notes would be shared and that everyone present for an interview had a responsibility to pay close attention. In some situations, two team members shared responsibility for note taking. This helped ensure that when team members were involved in formulating questions, they did not have to divide their attention between the interview process and recording the interview. In the community college RAP, interviews were recorded but note-taking responsibilities were still identified. The notes became critical when it was not possible to get the recordings of three interviews transcribed.

The experiences of the teams in Poland and with the community college convinced the members that some of their concerns about a team approach to data collection were unfounded. Being present for inquiries into areas outside the expertise of individual team members turned out not to be a "waste" of time. In Poland we may not have equally enjoyed trips to the swine production facilities, especially the one in a barn over one hundred years old; however, we all learned and were able to contribute to an understanding of how these facilities fit into the state farm system. Likewise, it was not an enjoyable experience for everyone on the team at the community college to sit through long accounts of problems with communication and the pain experienced by some of the participants. However, it was important to have the perspective of the different team members on this information. The insider on the community college team commented that each person on the team "displayed an admirable level of respect for the people being interviewed. I saw people whose behavior typically is full of hostility and mistrust open up on a real level. . . . What this project provided . . . was hope, for people to have a voice in a large, bureaucratic organization that typically does not honor individual voices, especially those of 'classified staff.' Members of both teams came to appreciate that several sets of eyes and ears and constant team interaction were essential for getting the most from the very short time spent in the field. Finally, our initial apprehensions about individual respondents feeling intimidated by a "gang of inquisitors" turned out not to be a problem, except in one case. Our sensitivity to this possibility helped prevent it from becoming an issue and helped us recognize the one situation where it was. Team interaction was absolutely critical for team productivity (see Changing the Role of Individual Team Members, p. 123).

Teamwork and Data Analysis

Iterative Data Collection and Analysis

> **Teams should meet every day.**

Teams usually met on those days when they did interviews. These meetings focused on what had been learned that day, what research strategies seemed to work best, and what should be done differently. In Poland, an effort was made to have the field notes typed each day, and a review of the field notes was often the starting point for the discussion. At the community college, transcripts were used as the beginning point for discussion. Specific attention was given to follow-up questions that needed to be asked and specific responsibility for asking these questions was often assigned.

The team paid close attention to contradictions and unexpected responses. During an initial group meeting with all of the directors of state farms in the regions, it was stated several times that all of the state farms were failing. When one of the first farms visited turned out to be doing well, the team began to focus on exceptions and to ask about them. A report on the devastating impact very high interest rates had on production loans led to an inquiry about the banking system and changes in the sources of finances for state farms. It quickly became apparent that under the old system the state advanced funds when needed and directors did not have to consider cash flow.

In Poland, in addition to the daily scheduled meetings, the team discussed various issues while traveling to and from interviews. After the first week of fieldwork, the team spent an entire Sunday afternoon reviewing the progress that was being made and changes that were needed.

Before the interviews with the directors of the last two of the ten state farms, the team met and made some initial decisions about responsibilities for the preparation of sections of the report. While it was obvious that, with only a few exceptions, state farm directors did not understand how a market economy was intended to operate, it was less obvious whether there were *specific* aspects of a market economy they did not understand. This was the first of several meetings in which we explored specific themes. Increased focus on a range of issues during the last few interviews helped the team reach consensus on five areas it identified as problematic for many state farm directors: (1) risk, (2) information, (3) production versus productivity, (4) price determination, and (5) cash-flow management.

The community college RAP team faced different issues requiring different approaches. After the first week of interviews, the team started the analysis process by dividing up the transcripts and letting individual team members begin the coding process. The team then met to discuss and list the codes that individuals had used. As a group, the team considered possible themes and developed several data displays that considered possible relationships of the themes. The first several interviews confirmed the impression of deep distrust left by the initial meeting with the leadership group from the Student Services Division. The team discussed strategies for exploring the extent to which the distrust was related to personality differences as opposed to structural issues. The interview guidelines were modified to ensure that information was collected on the length of service of individuals, the different roles they had held, and their experience with other institutions of higher education. From the first several interviews it was obvious to the team that there were serious differences in how individuals viewed the mission of the division and that some of these differences were related to differences between the unit responsible for general counseling and units responsible for providing services to students with special needs. The team considered ways of understanding these differences without making the situation worse. One response of the RAP team was to place more emphasis on getting participants to identify positive aspects of their work environment (see RAP and Appreciative Inquiry, p. 148). The community college RAP team faced three related problems that had to be discussed during the group meetings. The team believed that arrangements were in place to ensure that transcripts of interviews would be available the next day. After the first few days, the turnaround time for transcripts moved from overnight to several days. At the same time, the number of individuals who wanted to be interviewed increased dramatically, with several individuals requesting the opportunity to meet a second time with the RAP team. Delays in the production of transcripts and scheduling additional interviews pushed the process beyond the original schedule and team members began to run into schedule conflicts involving other things that they had planned prior to beginning the RAP.

In both cases, by the end of the fieldwork, the teams were spending as much or more time talking with each other and trying to make sense out of what was being observed as they were on observing new things. However, these discussions were interspersed with additional data collection. The teams used the additional data collection to resolve questions. The diversity of the teams and their ability to bring different disciplinary perspectives may have been more important for the iterative data analysis process than it was for the observation process. By the end of the RAP, there appeared to be genuine respect for the different technical expertise that team members brought to the discussion.

CHAPTER FOUR

Report Preparation and Additional Data Collection
The report preparation provided additional opportunities for team interaction and the identification of needs for additional data. Reviews of early drafts of the written sections by other team members led to corrections and new insights. In the Polish RAP, writing responsibilities were changed in two cases. Members of the community college RAP team distributed drafts to the other team members as e-mail attachments and, for making suggestions for changes in each other's work, used the "Highlight Changes" function in MS Word, under "Track Changes" on the "Tools" menu.

Even as the Poland team continued to gather data, they met with the local Ministry of Agriculture. At this meeting, the team presented their initial findings. There was general support for the findings regarding areas where directors of state farms misunderstood the requirements of a market economy, but open disagreement with the some of the initial recommendations of the team about how to address these issues. The ministry's concerns were worked into the report and the recommendations were modified.

Before the team left Poland, the English version of the final report was in draft. This version was left with the Polish member of the team so that he could start a translation into Polish. Once the English version was final, it was sent to the Polish member so that he could modify the Polish version to make it consistent with the English version. The Polish-speaking American member of the team reviewed the Polish version before it was released. Special effort was invested in trying to produce a report with a consistent message and ensuring that the English and Polish versions were identical in content. Gow argues that "a team that speaks with more than one voice is doomed" (Gow 1991, 12). While "doomed" may be an overstatement, the RAP team for the Polish study believed in the merit of trying to have the report speak with one voice, and made sure that adequate time was invested to realize this goal.

As noted above, the community college RAP team was not able to complete the final report as scheduled. Additional discussion of the factors that contributed to the delays is in chapter 6. This delay impacted the results of the RAP in at least three ways. As soon as the presentation on the initial findings had been made, but before the final report was submitted, the division began to address some of the issues. By the time the

88

final report was submitted, a plan was in place for organizing teams around the constraints identified by the report and limited funding was available to them. The RAP team recognized that changes in the wording of the report could contribute to this process without violating the integrity of the report. While the substance essentially remained the same, the tone became more positive. Finally, the delay gave the RAP team time to consider the interviews with two participants who had a very serious conflict with their supervisor. They had been especially concerned about confidentiality and feared repercussion. At the same time, they insisted on being interviewed. They made it clear to the "insider" on the team that they wanted input on the report. The RAP team concluded that, if very much of their input was included, they would be very easily identified, and that their issues were somewhat different from the issues of the other participants. A solution negotiated by the "insider" was a special presentation by the RAP team to the dean on these issues, which were then excluded from the report. I will return to this issue in the section below on the role of the "insider" on the team.

The explicit division of time between data collection and data analysis from the beginning of the fieldwork ensured that a mechanism was in place for sharing observations and interpretations. The identification of clear and complementary responsibilities for team members, and the presence of mechanisms for sharing observations and interpretations, were identified by Erickson and Stull (1998) as necessary for groups of researchers to function as a team. The structure of RAP ensures that these requirements are satisfied (see Team Membership, p. 24).

Outsiders and Insiders In-Between

Van Maanen et al. argue, "Any social group deserving of a label is one in which members in good standing are able to distinguish insiders from outsiders" (Van Maanen et al. 1996, v). These authors note that social research is based on efforts by investigators who have traditionally been outsiders trying to understand what the insiders believe, value, practice, and expect. While traditional research methodology has focused on helping the outsiders better understand the insiders' knowledge, there is a growing realization of the role the insiders should play in the design, implementation, and publication of research.

Van Maanen et al. also note that boundaries may be permeable, groups may overlap, and status can be relative, shifting, and ambiguous. This lack of clear definitions also applies to the identification of who is an insider for purposes of inclusion on the RAP team. It is desirable for the insider to be a member of the local group that is the subject of the RAP. However, sometimes the insider's role will be filled by someone from a neighboring organization or village who speaks the local language. In addition to language competency, at a minimum the insider needs to have had experiences similar to the ones most relevant to that being explored by the RAP.

The ability of RAP to begin the process over a short period of achieving an emic understanding of a situation requires the use of a team of researchers, with at least one team member an insider. Bartunek and Louis (1996) describe research conducted collaboratively by insiders and outsiders as involving the insiders in examining the setting and coauthoring any public accounts. They note that this includes having the insider involved in framing questions that guide the study and playing a role in the analysis of the data. Bartunek and Louis claim that "by capturing, conveying, and otherwise linking the perspectives and products of inquiry of both insiders and outsiders, a more robust picture can be produced of any particular phenomenon and setting under study" (11).

RAP depends upon having an insider on the team.

They further argue, "The more diverse the experience histories of the individuals composing a research team, especially in terms of their relationship to the setting, the more diverse should be their perspectives on and potential interpretations of any particular observed event there" (18).

The role of the insider on the RAP team is made more complex by the "action" objective of RAP of facilitating change in the setting under study. Bartunek and Louis (1996) suggest that where research has practical as well as scholarly ends, the insider can be expected to be motivated to improve his or her lot. They go on to say,

> If the outsider "goes native" or the insider "goes stranger," however, gains previously possible are compromised. . . . In identifying with insiders,

outsiders may be tempted to gloss over controversial issues in the setting that are pertinent to the study. In identifying with outsiders, insiders may be tempted to accept uncritically outsiders' categorizations for behavior, rather than contributing their own unique perspective. (56–57)

Bartunek and Louis (1996) identify several ethical challenges in conducting team research using both insiders and outsiders. Informed consent (discussed in more detail on p. 136, chapter 7) is made more problematic, since prospective participants cannot have full knowledge of what might come out of the research. The inability to know in advance what might develop is also a problem for the insider member of the team. Bartunek and Louis argue "a revised view of informed consent seems warranted, in which consent is negotiated at different points in the research cycle" (58). Confidentiality represents another ethical dilemma that is particularly relevant in presenting results of studies that include insiders as team members. Even when pseudonyms are used, there is a living link between quotes and individuals. Where the decision is made not to identify the site of the study, the institutional affiliation of the insider will often identify the site.

Initial plans for the Polish RAP did not include explicit reference to the involvement of insiders. According to Bartunek and Louis (1996) this is not unusual for teams that eventually include insiders. The Polish agricultural engineer was clearly an insider for the agricultural sector of Poland. While he had experience with state farms, he was not an insider for the state farm community in Koszalin province. From the initial meeting with the American team, he was considered a full member of the team.

Urszula Golebiowska, the chief specialist for economics and transformation in the Ministry of Agriculture for Koszalin, was very much an insider to the state farm community in Koszalin. She joined the team for almost all of the visits to the state farms. In addition to providing introductions for the rest of the team, she answered questions from the other team members and ensured that the team did not overlook critical issues.

The demands of his job prevented Jansz Turski, the director of the Koszalin office of the Ministry of Agriculture, from participating in as much of the team efforts as he would have liked. His contributions were especially significant at the beginning and the end of the fieldwork. At the beginning of the work, he suggested areas of concern and identified opportunities for the team to participate in events that were already planned, such as a meeting of all the directors of state farms in the region. His greatest impact, however, was at the end of the process. The rest of the team benefited from being able to explore preliminary ideas about areas where state farm directors had the greatest misunderstanding of a market economy. Turski communicated to the rest of the team the need to identify specific recommendations and to clearly define an explicit role for the ministry. He was responsible for arranging meetings between the team and the leadership of the local ministry and provincial official. These meetings were critical for the productivity of the iterative process.

The role of the insiders in this RAP activity contributed to the ability of the team to produce the timely results that had been requested. Because of their self-interest in the results, the insiders helped ensure that the results made sense and that recommendations could be implemented. Finally, their presence helped with the implementation of the recommendations. The ministry used the results to begin refocusing their training. They also used their involvement in the research to facilitate the assignment of two USDA agricultural systems specialists to the Ministry of Agriculture.

The community college RAP was designed to include an insider as a full team member. She was the first team member identified and she played an informal role in the selection of the other members. Because of her longer experience at the college than the new dean, she was in a position to provide advice on the types of individuals who would be most appropriate. Her status as a student in the same doctoral program as the other team members contributed to her acceptance by the team as a full member. Because she was obviously respected by her community college colleagues, she was able to allay their concerns about confidentiality and reinforce the rationale for the study. Participants were explicitly asked whether they had concerns about her presence during the interviews; no one did.

Despite trying to remember which "hat" she wore at work during the RAP and to act accordingly, some of her colleagues refused to differentiate between her as "the faculty member" and her as "the RAP team member." Some of the demands of her colleagues caused role conflict. She wrote, "For example, I was perceived as being 'favored' by the dean simply because I was chosen to work on the study. Given my 'favored' status, a few assumed I knew more about the dean and her motives than anybody else. 'How well do you know her?' I was asked on more than one occasion." When it became obvious that not everyone wishing to be interviewed could be, she was the one who explained the situation and listened to the complaints.

Her role as the insider caught between the local situation and the outside team is best illustrated by her involvement with the participants who wanted to be interviewed but were extremely concerned about the possibility of retribution. They approached her, asking to be included. She then had to reassure them about what would be done to protect their confidentiality, while at the same time cautioning them that, although the team would make its best effort, confidentiality could not be "guaranteed." She listened to their concerns about having the transcripts of their interviews transcribed by anyone associated with the college, and the team made arrangements to have them transcribed by someone not associated. She provided input to the rest of the team on the materials from their interviews that were so specific to their situation as to make their source obvious. When most of these participants' concerns were not included in the report, it was the insider on the team whom they approached with a request to have information shared with the dean, but not included in the report. The insider negotiated the arrangement between the dean and the team for the oral presentation focusing on the concerns of these two participants. The insider understood their sense of urgency and made sure that the meeting occurred. She also made sure that the two participants knew it had happened.

After the rest of the team has moved on, the insider still has to deal with the consequences of the RAP.

Even when the rest of the RAP team had gone on to other things, the insiders continued to be called upon to clarify results, resolve pending issues, and help organize local responses to the results. The community college insider has been asked to predict the outcomes of impending changes in the organization structure and to "read the mind" of the dean about critical issues. She was told information that her colleagues implied she should "share" with the dean. She wrote, "When I pointedly sat silent with no offer to run to the Dean with what I was being told outside of the RAP interviews, I was met with looks of disappointment, as if I were committing betrayal." She was also aware of avoiding situations where she might be perceived "as taking advantage of information gained through the RAP process." Despite what she identified as the "cultural landmines" resulting from her role as an insider on the RAP team, she was emphatic that she would repeat the process if given the opportunity.

Team Leadership

RAP depends upon teamwork, and teamwork to some extent depends upon team leadership. I have witnessed the situation described by Erickson and Stull and have seen the frustration it can produce:

> Administrative inexperience, often combined with reluctance to lead, are common problems for research teams. Academics by and large do not like structured work settings and often rebel against hierarchy. (Erickson and Stull 1998, 30)

Teamwork depends on leadership.

Leadership should not be confused with either the exercise of control or the use of power. Heifetz discusses an approach to leadership that is especially relevant to RAP. He calls this approach "adaptive leadership." The first objective of the adaptive leader is to give individuals involved in a complex situation the opportunity to participate in finding solutions to their own problems (Heifetz 1994, 85). Heifetz identifies several other principles of adaptive leadership relevant to RAP, including providing "holding environments" (66), identifying adaptive challenges, and keeping distress within a productive range (207). According to Heifetz, the adaptive leader uses authority to construct relationships in which the participants raise, process, and resolve tough questions for which there are no obvious answers (85).

RAP teams must be more structured than the loose alliance model that has characterized traditional qualitative research. Under the loose alliance model, fieldworkers may work on individual projects and may write up findings separately (Erickson and Stull 1998, 14). Team leadership is especially important for structuring teams and maintaining the structure. The relative status of team members can undermine team structure. Erickson and Stull caution that team members of similar professional status and age may balk at formalized organizational structure and defined roles (15).

The extent of prior experience with teamwork needs to be considered in determining how much structure is needed. Teams with less experience might do better with more directive leadership. The key is that there must be some clear sense of organization.

I am convinced that the five most critical responsibilities of the team leader are (1) providing orientation, (2) keeping the activity focused and responsive to changing conditions, (3) maintaining morale, (4) team building, and (5) ensuring that administrative support is provided.

Orientation for RAP requires convincing the team that the success of the effort requires close teamwork to compensate for the lack of time in the field. The difference in the amount of time spent on a RAP relative to a traditional study can be shocking to traditional researchers. One member of the Polish team suggested that he had spent a longer time designing his last study than the RAP team spent doing the study and completing the report. For team members without formal training in qualitative research, the most important message is that the objective in interviewing people is to get them to tell stories and not just provide answers to questions. Orientation for the language interpreters involved both telling them what was expected and then practicing with team members. Anytime the translation seemed shorter than the original response we were suspicious. The Polish-speaking American team members were given the responsibility of ensuring that rich responses survived the translation process (see Orientation, p. 119).

The success of RAP depends upon maintaining balance between focus and flexibility. The team leader has a special responsibility for ensuring that interview guidelines and critical issues are not ignored, unless the team makes an explicit decision to change them. However, the team leader shares responsibility with the rest of the team to ensure that unexpected issues that come up receive the attention they deserve. For the Polish RAP, it was my responsibility to ensure that the success stories from some of the state farms were kept in perspective and that the team did not spend a disproportionate amount of time investigating some fascinating efforts to develop tourist facilities that had little relevance for most state farms in Poland. Responsibility for maintaining balance between focus and flexibility was shared by the entire team for the community college RAP.

The team leader responsibilities for maintaining morale and team building are related. For the Polish RAP, morale depended upon moderating the pace of activities before the team killed the leader. Scheduling time for team members to be away from the team and arranging some work-related tourist events helped. Thompson states, "My most constant and difficult role turned out to be that of morale builder. . . . Someone has to keep up the morale of the group" (Thompson 1970, 60). Differences in experience and status imposed a special burden on the team-building effort. Even if more-experienced team members value the contributions of less-experienced members, the less-experienced members may doubt their contributions. An important aspect of team building was communicating the message that the contribution of all team members was valued.

To ensure that maximum time is available for data collection and iterative data collection and analysis, logistics have to be worked out (see Logistics—Keeping RAP from Becoming SAP, p. 119). Someone has to arrange for vehicles, housing, and meals when the team has to travel to conduct the RAP. The Polish RAP team brought their own laptop computer, but local arrangements had to be made for a printer and paper. One of the major issues the community college RAP team faced was delay in the preparation of transcripts of the taped interviews. I will return to this logistical problem in chapter 7, when I discuss the responsibilities of the sponsors versus the RAP team.

The leader is responsible for ensuring that the administrative needs of the team are met but does not necessarily have to do it himself or herself. The Polish team was fortunate in being able to arrange for the services of an individual who did an excellent job in this area.

Teamwork and the Success of a RAP

RAP depends on intensive teamwork to compensate for the short amount of time spent on fieldwork. The experiences of the teams in Poland and at the community college suggest that this can be accomplished successfully.

There are numerous issues that influence the productivity of teams. Among the more important issues are the organization and structure of the multidisciplinary team, the team leadership, and the roles of insiders on the team.

The next chapter explores issues concerning the extent to which RAP can be trusted. Some of the charges against RAP can be answered, but there are other concerns that are not so easy to deal with. Keeping RAP flexible while also keeping it rigorous is an issue that can be addressed. No one should trust the results of a RAP unless the local people trust the RAP team. At the end of the next chapter, I will return to the issue of bad RAP and good RAP, and you would be disappointed if I did not raise once more the issue of RAP done too quickly. I will not disappoint you.

Additional Readings

Much of the conceptual material in this chapter is based on Bartunek and Louis (1996) and Erickson and Stull (1998). Heifetz's (1994) book provides an excellent introduction to the leadership style I believe is most relevant to successful RAP.

Bartunek, J. M., and M. R. Louis. 1996. *Insider/outsider research*. Thousand Oaks, Calif.: Sage.

Erickson, K., and D. Stull. 1998. *Doing team ethnography: Warnings and advice*. Thousand Oaks, Calif.: Sage.

Heifetz, R. D. 1994. *Leadership without easy answers*. Cambridge, Mass.: Belknap.

TRUSTING RAP

Main Points

1. At the heart of the question on whether to trust the results of a RAP is deciding whether RAP is an appropriate methodology for a specific situation.

2. For most situations, RAP should produce a sufficiently rich understanding of the insider's perspective for the design of additional research or for initiating activities that should be started promptly.

3. Spending too little time on the RAP is the most serious threat to its rigor. If done too quickly and without sufficient methodological rigor, RAP can be more dangerous than "research tourism."

4. Gender diversity may be vital in establishing the credibility and trustworthiness of the team with community members.

5. The RAP team should seek out the poorer, the less articulate, the more upset, and those least like the members of the RAP team, and it should involve them in both data collection and analysis.

6. Usually, rapid research methods should not be used for estimating numbers or percents of a population with specific characteristics.

7. Calling research methods rapid has been used to justify and legitimize sloppy, biased, and rushed work.

8. Flexibility is critical to making RAP relevant to a wide range of systems and is a major strength of the approach. However, this flexibility can be abused.

9. Use the "RAP sheet" to document what was done and to allow the reader to judge the quality of the work.

Trust and RAP

Before anyone embraces RAP as a methodology, she or he needs answers to the following questions:

Is RAP too quick for doing ethnographic inquiry?
Does RAP reduce support for more appropriate research methodology?
What are the legitimate concerns about RAP and can they be addressed?
What can be done to make RAP both flexible and rigorous?
What makes good RAP into bad RAP?

At the heart of the question on whether to trust RAP is deciding whether RAP is an appropriate methodology for a specific situation. If a situation is appropriate for RAP, the next questions concern the rigor with which the methodology is applied. Not everything called RAP is RAP and Chambers (1996) cautions about "cosmetic labeling without substance."

RAP, the Insider's Perspective, and Time in the Field

Almost all descriptions of ethnography refer to a requirement for prolonged periods in the field. (Creswell 1998; Erickson and Stull 1998; Miles and Huberman 1994; Wolcott 1987, 1995; Bernard 1995). Wolcott (1995) discusses fieldwork as intimate, long-term acquaintance. He notes that the previous ideal of two years or longer in the field as the standard has been shortened to twelve months, but that few can afford to spend even this much time in the field. Wolcott argues that a minimum of twelve months of fieldwork is often needed if one is to be present through a full cycle of activity. He notes that the early anthropologists studied people through the cycle related to the annual growing seasons. The need to gain access and establish rapport has been noted as justification for prolonged fieldwork, as has the need to observe normal situations, reflective of the everyday life of individuals, groups, societies, and organizations. The down side of prolonged fieldwork can be the volume of data collected. My own experience was that the almost one year I spent in the field for my dissertation research resulted in something that can best be described as "**social**

science voyeurism." Social science voyeurism involves making inquiries on human behavior and practices to satisfy curiosity beyond what is needed or can be used.

Despite the widespread identification of ethnography with prolonged fieldwork, there are occasional references to the possibility that ethnography can be done in less time. Anthropologists including Robert Redfield, Sol Tax, James Spradley, David McCurdy, Penn Handwerker, and Margaret Mead have either described or defended rapid ethnographic methods.

There is an unfortunate tendency to equate time with quality and to dismiss quick results with terms like "quick and dirty." Even researchers like Wolcott with valid concerns about the quality of "quick" results concede that "time in the field is no guarantee of the quality of the ensuing report" (1995, 110). The case for prolonged fieldwork is based on the arguments that (1) it takes time to develop intellectualized competence in another culture (Bernard 1995, 140, 150), (2) it takes time to be accepted and to develop rapport with the locals and this is related to being able to cover more sensitive topics (Bernard 1995, 140), (3) it takes time to be included in gossip, (4) it takes time to get information about social change, and (5) it is the traditional way of doing fieldwork (Wolcott 1995). There is a degree of validity to the first four of these arguments. They may, however, be more valid concerns for "quick and dirty" methods than they are for RAP.

The argument on the need for time to develop intellectualized competence in another culture rests on two assumptions. The first is that fieldwork will be done in an exotic location where the researcher does not speak the native language and has not picked up the "nuances of etiquette" from previous experience (Bernard 1995, 140). This may or may not be true for any qualitative research, including a RAP. Even as Bernard argues for extended time in the field, he identifies the laundromat as the type of place where one with previous experience in laundromats could conduct a reasonable participant observation study in a week. I would argue that this same argument would hold for public health experts trying to examine factors associated with risky sexual behavior in their own country, educators looking at the organizational culture in a school, or Thai aquaculture experts interested in constraints to a proposed way of managing fish ponds. In each of these cases, the individuals may be facing a complex situation in which, despite their knowledge of the local language and etiquette, they do not know the categories used by the individuals most closely involved in the system to describe the specific situation. If the assumption is valid that the locale for the research is an exotic location, then the second assumption comes into play. It is the researcher who must develop intellectualized competence. RAP is based on the full participation of local insiders as team members, and the assumption is that they bring knowledge of the language and etiquette. The use of the local team members and the careful and thoughtful use of language interpreters as outlined in chapter 2 can help address this problem. Bernard (1995, 140) notes that when Chambers is called on to do rapid assessment of rural village needs, he takes the people fully into his confidence as research partners.

The argument on the need for extended time to develop rapport is based on three assumptions that may not be relevant to RAP. The first is that deep rapport based on extended interaction is necessary to deal with sensitive topics, like sexual behaviors and political feuds. Usually a RAP is done in response to an identified need or problem. Because of the topic focus of the RAP and the shared concern about the topic at the local level, there is usually a willingness to discuss it. My experience has been that cooperation can be expected if local people recognize that outsiders are genuinely interested in working with them to address their problems. The second assumption is that it always takes time to develop rapport. My experience is that personalities and shared interests are more important for establishing rapport than the length of time people spend with each other. Diversity on the RAP team increases the possibilities that there will be individuals who by nature are able to develop rapport quickly and that there will be similarities between team members and local people. Finally, the third assumption is that, without extended periods to develop rapport, the team using a rapid approach is limited to "going in and getting on with the job of collecting data" and that this means "going into a field situation armed with a list of questions that you want to answer and perhaps a checklist of data that you need to collect" (Bernard 1995, 139). RAP explicitly is based on getting more than the answers to questions prepared in advance. The assumption for RAP is that enough cannot be known in advance to formulate these types of questions. The acrimonious relationship between some anthropologists and the local people, as evidenced by harassment and assaults, suggests that prolonged time in the field does not always equate to the development of rapport (see also Lee 1994).

One of the arguments for extended fieldwork is that it takes time to be included in gossip. The assumption is that especially valuable information will likely come from informal interviews in which informants gossip freely. Anyone who believes it takes a prolonged period to gain access to gossip has never had the opportunity of taking an elevator ride with my late mother. The sharing of gossip almost always encourages the production of gossip.

The assumption that without extended fieldwork there will not be an opportunity for interaction between researchers and local people outside the formal research structure does not hold for RAPs. The inclusion of locals as full partners on the team and the intensive interaction of those locals with other members of the team, both while collecting data and during the iterative data collection/data analysis process, ensure opportunities for informal gossip.

The view that it takes extended periods of time to get information about social change assumes that only very long-term participant observation can get at changes over several decades. This assumption appears to consider only the length of a single, initial period of fieldwork and to ignore returns to the field to conduct follow-up studies. Not only is there nothing that precludes additional RAPs a decade after the first one, follow-up RAPs are probably more likely to occur than additional traditional research, since the critical resource limiting the return to the field by traditional researchers is often their lack of time for prolonged fieldwork.

There is some recognition that "traditions" are one source of the contention by some that extended time in the field is required for research. Wolcott notes:

> To an old-time and old-fashioned ethnographer like me, terms like *ethnography* or *fieldwork* join uneasily with a qualifier like *rapid*. . . . My motto, to 'do less, more thoroughly,' may be nothing more than rationalization for my preferred and accustomed pace. Perhaps I envision a fieldwork entirely of my own making, having mistakenly accepted pronouncement about its duration (such as 'one year at the least, and preferably two') as minimum standards when today's fieldworkers regard them as impractical and unnecessary. (1999, 110)

There may be some situations in which prolonged fieldwork is required to gain access and build rapport, in which situations are extremely complex, or a long cycle needs to be monitored. However, for most situations, RAP should produce a sufficiently rich understanding of the insider perspective for the design of additional research or to initiate activities that have to be started quickly.

> For many situations, RAP should provide enough of the insiders' perspectives to initiate activities or additional research.

Despite the strong case that prolonged fieldwork often is not required to achieve the goals of ethnography, many anthropologists can be expected to remain skeptical of the rapidity of RAPs. As long as they conceive of RAP as a one-off exercise by outsiders who lack an initial understanding and familiarity with the environment, they are likely to view any information or knowledge gained from RAP as superficial (Leurs 1997, 292). My goal is to help anyone with these concerns understand the role of intensive teamwork and especially the role of insiders as members of the team in a RAP.

RAP and Support for Long-Term Fieldwork

As long as people have been doing rapid research, others have been suggesting that the real danger is that the rapid work is being done instead of the long-term work that is needed. The implication is that the rapid approaches are chosen because they are cheaper and that if they were not available, these resources could be used for prolonged fieldwork. Some fear RAP will undermine support for less glamorous work (Abate 1992, 486). The problem with this argument is that it assumes that there is time for long-term work. In many cases where RAP is used, results are needed immediately to design interventions for problems that will not wait. Often it is not a question of doing rapid versus long-term fieldwork. The option of long-term fieldwork is not there. In some cases there might be time to do more prolonged fieldwork, but the resources are not there. Carrying out a RAP is not as cheap as some assume, but it is almost always cheaper than conventional, long-term work. Where time and resources are limited, the alternatives are either no inquiry (and research tourism is not counted as inquiry) or to do inappropriate research, such as questionnaire survey research, because it is believed to be quick.

RAP can complement long-term research.

Rapid research can complement long-term research in situations where the time and funding are available. One of the goals of RAP is to identify when further research is needed. A RAP can identify situations where longer qualitative work is needed to establish rapport, deal with extremely complex issues, or monitor a long-term process like a growing season or language acquisition by a child. RAP can also provide the categories and terms to make questionnaire research meaningful in situations where categories and specific terms used by local people are not known. Many of the advocates of RAP agree with Emmons, a research associate at the Smithsonian Institution, that whenever possible RAP is intended to supplement, not replace, long-term field work (Abate 1992, 487).

Concerns about RAP

The following concerns affect people's trust in the results of RAP or limit its usefulness. In some cases, there is not much that can be done about a concern, but in most cases knowing about it will allow the RAP team to address it.

Too Little or Too Much Time

Even though I am convinced ethnographic inquiry can be done quickly, I am also convinced that there is a minimum time requirement. Two points should be emphasized. One, more time in the field will inevitably produce better results, with the possibility of some limited exceptions discussed below. Two, spending too little time on the RAP is the most serious threat to its rigor. Team members need sufficient time to be observant, sensitive, and eclectic (Carruthers and Chambers 1981, 418). Attempts at RAP carried out with insufficient time and inadequate planning should probably be called "research tourism." One of my students suggested another name (one with an appropriate acronym) for RAP done too quickly would be

Condensed Rapid Assessment Process. Inadequate time introduces predictable biases into the process, including inappropriate focus on elements of the situation that are most obvious, observation of situations when it is physically easiest to observe, contact with individuals already involved in change, and contact with individuals who are less disadvantaged (Chambers 1980, 3). Inadequate time can also result in not enough attention to the relationships, may result in a failure to recognize that what is seen is a moment in time and is not necessarily the long-term trend. The length of a RAP will depend upon the situation, but anything less than four days is probably inadequate for carrying out discussions; identifying, discussing, modifying, and rejecting ideas that emerge from these discussions; and putting these ideas together in a usable form.

> **Less than four days is probably inadequate!**

There are some situations where results must be produced in a timely way if they are to be useful. Additional field time might improve the precision but would make the results useless. When resources are limited, the choice might be between having a lone researcher for a longer period or a team for a shorter period of time. In some cases shorter fieldwork by a team may be more useful than longer-term research by a lone researcher. Complex situations may require the expertise of several disciplines. There are also isolated situations in which additional time in the field communicates the wrong message about the confidence one can have in the results. Longer fieldwork may result in increased confidence in the results, when healthy skepticism is appropriate. Finally, a RAP that is too long may waste time and cause both insiders and outsiders to view the RAP as an end in itself, instead of as a tool for starting the learning process.

Cultural Appropriateness

The fundamental role of teams and the inclusion of local people on these teams may make RAP culturally inappropriate for some situations. Given the public nature of much RAP work, one should expect serious distortions in cultures where women do not participate openly in public life. Mixed-gender teams may be especially inappropriate for some topics and may have an inhibiting effect on the participation of some (Leurs

1997, 292). The RAP teams should be especially sensitive to the cultural appropriateness of using techniques like rich picture with people more comfortable with telling stories, rankings with people reluctant to compare each other, or tape recorders in a wide range of situations.

Political and Economic Context

An accurate assessment of a situation should include a full description of the context. According to Manderson and Aaby (as cited in Harris, Jerome, and Fawcett 1997, 376), rapid research methods often consider the social and cultural context, but do not consider the political and economic context. Consideration of the political and economic context is closely tied to issues of differences in power and the relationship between the sponsors, the local stakeholders, and the RAP team. I will return to this issue in chapter 7.

Problems with Team Composition

For the results of RAP to be useful, the assessment team must be credible. Using multidisciplinary teams in RAP generally increases credibility. The lack of gender diversity on many teams continues to be a problem. Gender diversity may be vital in establishing the credibility and trustworthiness of the team with community members (Harris et al. 1997, 376).

For RAP to work, team members need solid experience in their respective disciplines. "People have to be experienced to do RAP. Only when [researchers] know how to do it right can they do it fast" (Abate 1992, 486). There is some concern that the shortage of support for long-term studies may tempt funding agencies to let less-experienced researchers undertake rapid assessments before they have proven themselves in traditional scientific field work (486). Even though RAP teams need members with both technical expertise in their discipline and an understanding of qualitative research, the success of RAP does not depend upon "superstars." I do not accept Macintyre's (1995) argument that a serious weakness of rapid research is its dependence for quality on the caliber of the expert team members. Assuming team members have an adequate level of technical expertise, they should be able to develop sufficient understanding of the principles of qualitative research to be able to select appropriate research techniques. Given the right attitude, with practice these skills should improve, especially if attention is given to identifying lessons from the implementation of each RAP.

Problems with Choice of Respondents and Informants

It is often easy to find people to talk with who are better off, more articulate, and more like the members of the RAP team. It is far more difficult to find the poorer, less articulate, and more upset, and those least like the members of the RAP team, and to involve them in both data collection and analysis. The RAP sheet has been designed to remind the team of the need for diversity in whom they talk to, including finding and talking to the "trouble makers." Chambers (1996) suggests that you ask yourself, "who is being met and heard, and what is being seen, and where and why; and who is not being met and heard, and what is not being seen, and where and why?"

Inappropriate Use

Rapid research methods are not appropriate for some situations. Usually, rapid research methods should not be used for estimating numbers or percents of a population with specific characteristics. It is therefore not very surprising that an Expanded Programme of Immunization study in Nigeria suggested an immunization rate of approximately 80 percent, while a demographic and health survey found a rate of only 50 percent for the same age children. A statistician commenting on the Nigerian results said that it was his opinion that "health managers are only fooling themselves if they rely on this methodology for estimates of coverage." Sampling procedures and the lack of trustworthy data on households to sample are some of the problems with the use of rapid research to estimate numbers (Macintyre 1995, 5).

Problems with Credibility

Chambers (1996) laments that calling research methods rapid has "been used to justify and legitimize sloppy, biased, rushed, and unself-critical work." Despite the large number of rapid research reports that have been done during the last several decades, there has been very little criticism of methods by practitioners. This type of criticism is needed to improve the methodology and increase the credibility of the results. Chambers advises, "Embrace error. We all make mistakes, and do things badly sometimes. . . . Don't hide it. Share it." (see the Need for Caution about the Use of RAP, p. 14)

The credibility of RAP and other rapid research methods would increase if there were empirical evidence to test rapid assessment results against more conventional methods. Macintyre (1995) notes the lack of such evidence and suggests the case for rapid research methods is still tentative. He notes, however, that there are positive signs of interest in experimentation with faster, cheaper methods. There is also a lack of evidence that the RAP process has had impact on project design or program functioning. Harris et al. (1997, 376) note that they are not aware of any published reports on the impact of rapid research methods on programs. Practitioners of these methods have a responsibility to report on conventional studies that confirm or deny the results of RAP as well as its impact on programs.

The limited publication of the results of rapid research methods in peer-reviewed journals is an issue for some observers. Despite the presence of four world-renowned scientists on one of the early RAPs by Conservation International, the credibility of their results was questioned because they did not publish them in a peer-reviewed journal (Abate 1992, 486). The response of one of the team members, Ted Parker, was "Ten or 15 years from now our scientific contributions won't be important, but there may be some places that still exist because of what we've done" (486). Peer review of the results of RAP by colleagues is desirable and is encouraged. Publishing results in peer-reviewed journals is one, but not the only, way to achieve this. Peer-reviewed journals that have published articles based on rapid research methods (see Sharing RAP Reports, p. 127) include:

African Journal of Ecology (UK)
Agricultural Systems (UK)
BioScience (US)
British Medical Journal (UK)
High Plains Applied Anthropologist (US)
Human Organization (US)
International Information and Library Review (UK)
Journal of International Agricultural and Extension Education (US)
Landscape and Urban Planning (Netherlands)
Rural Society (Australia)

CHAPTER FIVE

Rural Sociology (US)
Tropical Medicine and International Health (UK)

Many of the rapid assessment procedures were developed in response to calls from funding agencies for faster ethnographic field research (Kumar 1987). While these methods have been recognized by many in the donor community as vital for in-depth understanding of problems, there are still some who are uncomfortable with them. One of the most frequently identified problems with rapid research methods is that they do not produce numbers. Usually, if numbers are needed, RAP is an inappropriate method, especially if it is to be used alone. Funding agencies need to recognize that there are many situations in which an understanding of a local situation using the terms and categories of the local participants is sufficient for the initial design of an intervention. There are other times when the results of RAP will be critical for the design of additional research or for monitoring the implementation of activities. Practitioners have a responsibility to resist pressure from funding organizations to use rapid methods in inappropriate situations. If rapid methods are used in inappropriate situations, the results will be subject to valid criticism.

Dealing with Flexibility

One of the major challenges for RAP is to sustain and enhance inventiveness and creativity with new methods, and with combinations and sequences of techniques, without losing rigor. Flexibility is critical to making RAP relevant to a wide range of systems and is a major strength of the approach. However, this flexibility can be abused and has been interpreted by some as allowing individuals to do anything, or almost nothing, and call it "RAP." A set of standard techniques could solve this problem, but only at the expense of the needed flexibility. One of the most common criticisms of rapid assessment methods has been their arbitrary "laundry-list type elements" (Anker 1991 cited in Macintyre 1995). The alternative to standardization is agreement on basic principles and then documentation, as part of the RAP report, of the specific techniques used. I propose the use of a checklist, the "RAP sheet," to document what was done and to allow the reader to judge the quality of the work. The checklist also can remind the RAP team of important issues during the appraisal.

Sample RAP Sheet

The generic checklist below should be adapted to the specific situation of each RAP. It is very unlikely that all the items on the sample RAP sheet will be relevant to any specific RAP, and even if they are it could make the checklist too long to be useful. The RAP sheet is loosely based on the Human Relations Area Files data quality control schedule (Lagacé 1970).

Modify first and then use the RAP Sheet.

Bad RAP and Good RAP

If done too quickly and without sufficient methodological rigor, RAP can be more dangerous than "research tourism." At a minimum there is a need for team orientation, and for several cycles of data collection and analysis. Triangulation for data collection requires at a minimum time for multiple semistructured interviews and for careful observations that are most relevant to the situation being investigated. An iterative approach to data collection and analysis requires time for the team to meet, to carefully consider what it has found, to develop and consider data displays, and to explore tentative conclusions before returning to the field for additional data collection. Checking back with the individuals who have provided information takes time, as does the preparation of a report.

When there is not enough time to do RAP rigorously, it is less dangerous to do "research tourism" and to clearly identify it as such. Decisions based on poor data are no more likely to be good decisions than decisions based on no data at all (Macintyre 1995).

RAP provides relatively quick qualitative results that are likely to be sound enough that they can be used for decisions about additional research or preliminary decisions for the design and implementation of applied activities. When applied with care and caution, RAP can help prevent the errors that can result from "tourism" or the inappropriate use of a questionnaire survey before a local situation is sufficiently well understood to formulate questions. I am not suggesting that RAP can substitute for long-term, in-depth studies, where a situation calls for that and time and resources are available. I am suggesting that, in many situations, RAP will

RAP Sheet

Title:[1]
Objectives:
Fieldwork dates:
Report completion date:
RAP team members

Name	Tech. Background	Language Use[2]	Local/Outsider[3]	RAP Experience[4]

Number of hours spent in field collecting data:
Number of hours spent by team in discussing data:
Information collected in advance and reviewed by the team:
Types of information collected by direct observation:
Number of individual respondents interviewed:
Method of selection of respondents:
Place of interviews:
Among individual respondents, approximately what percent were from different groups relevant to the system being investigated?

_____% women, _____% old people, _____% youth
_____% from among the poorest 25 percent
_____% from among the 25 percent who live farthest from the road
_____% from significant ethnic or cultural minorities
_____% from those identified as troublemakers

Number of key informants interviewed:
Method of selecting key informants, their positions/occupation, and topics they reported on:
Topics for group interviews and composition of groups:
Date set for reviewing and updating this report:

---

[1]The title should include the name of the geographic or administrative unit.
[2]Language use categories:
A. Exclusive use of respondents first language
B. Use of respondents' second language
C. Mixture of respondents' first and second languages
D. Mixture of respondents' languages and use of interpreter
E. Exclusive use of interpreters
[3]Local or outsider categories:
A. From site, living and working there
B. From outside the area
[4]Categories for prior experience
N. No prior experience doing RAP
T. Participation in a training course on RAP
Number of prior RAP.

Figure 5.1 Sample RAP Sheet

produce sufficiently solid results for the design of additional research or to initiate activities that have to be started promptly.

Experience with RAP suggests that special attention to a limited number of specific issues can improve the quality of the process. The next chapter highlights eighteen specific suggestions based on materials in earlier chapters. I recognize that some of these suggestions reiterate what has been said, but I believe they are so critical to success that they should be repeated. Since in some ways chapter 6 is a summary of the main points of the book, the chapter does not start with a separate section of main points. It is unlikely that every suggestion will be relevant to a specific RAP, and in some cases the success of the RAP may depend upon ignoring specific suggestions. Flexibility and being comfortable with ambiguity are essential to RAP.

CHAPTER SIX
SUCCESSFUL RAP

Integrating Intensive Teamwork and Maintaining Flexibility

It is the intensive teamwork associated with the basic concepts of triangulation, and iterative analysis and additional data collection, and not a list of specific research techniques, that defines RAP and differentiates it from other approaches to research. It is the intensive teamwork that allows the process to be rapid. Even though there are research techniques associated with RAP and the basic concepts that have proven effective under a range of conditions, these are not the only techniques that can be used. Since RAP is not defined by a specific set of techniques, there is real flexibility in the process. Factors that influence how a specific RAP will be implemented include, first and foremost, the team. Not only the technical expertise of the team members must be considered, but their previous experience with research and, especially, with qualitative research. Prior experience working as team members and attitudes toward collaborative work may be as important as previous experience doing qualitative research.

> While specific techniques have proven effective for RAP, these are NOT the only ones that can be used.

The flexibility in the choice of research techniques means that a technique can be chosen because a team member has experience using it. If a team member is a skilled photographer, the RAP might make extensive use of photos. If a team member is skilled in the use of spreadsheets and financial systems, she could be expected to open lines of inquiry in these areas. Artists/graphic designers could be called upon to help respondents with the creation of rich pictures and to help the team with data displays as part of the data analysis process. There are yet to be explored roles for musicians and dramatists on RAP teams. Given that the objective of semistructured interviewing is to get the respondent to "tell a story," there may be roles on the team for storytellers to both encourage and help make sense out of these stories. The use of metaphors for data analysis may make the individual with a literary background one of the most important members of the team.

Sensitivity to cultural differences is essential.

Sensitivity to cultural differences is absolutely necessary on the RAP team. The need for sensitivity should be recognized by the team and nurtured. It should not be assumed that sensitivity to cultural differences is associated with a specific discipline or ethnic group. Someone on the team must always be able and willing to question the cultural implications of decisions. The types of situations where cultural sensitivity might be especially relevant include the identification of topics that can be discussed in public, the use of drawings, the role of elders, and the use of focus group interviews as opposed to individual, semistructured interviews.

The prior experience of team members should be carefully considered. RAP teams that include members with more experience in qualitative research, teamwork, and RAP will need less-explicit guidance on the selection of techniques (Grandstaff and Grandstaff 1987, 87). As discussed in chapter 4, teams with less experience may need a different type of leadership than teams with more experience.

The rest of this chapter contains a somewhat arbitrary list of suggestions for making RAP more successful. Obviously, not all of the suggestions apply to every RAP. Where appropriate, page numbers are given, so more information can be found on specific topics.

Before Beginning to RAP

Attitude

Attitude is everything for the RAPper. The ability to embrace ambiguity and collaborative approaches may be more important than the technical expertise and experience of team members. Attitudes should be carefully considered in team selection. Identifying and encouraging positive attitudes should be part of the orientation and a priority for the team leader throughout the process. The three attitudes that may be most critical for successful RAP are recognizing (1) you don't know enough to ask questions, (2) you don't know enough to provide the answers, but (3) you do know enough to want to empower others to solve their own problems. Chambers (1996) cautions against assuming we know what to ask and notes that "the beginning of wisdom is to realize how often we do not know what we do not know." As noted several times before, the complexity of most situations and our inability to know the categories and terms used by local people make getting people to tell stories more important than getting them to answer questions. If we do not know enough to be able to ask the right questions, we certainly do not know enough to impose our ideas. Yet Chambers (1996) notes that, often, teams impose their ideas, solutions, categories, and values without realizing they are doing it and that this makes it difficult for them to learn from the others. The third critical attitude is one that sustains and embraces sharing and lateral learning and is based on the assumption that finding solutions often depends upon empowering others to solve their own problems. For some "experts" who view their role as problem solving, this requires a fundamental change in attitude.

RAPpers need to recognize:

(1) they don't know enough to ask questions,

(2) they don't know enough to provide the answers, but

(3) they do know enough to want to empower others to solve their own problems.

Chambers (1996) refers to the empowerment of the weak, women, and the poor "to take part more and more and to gain more and more." If attitudes are neglected, the **local community** ceases being the partner of the RAP team and there is a danger that the process will become mechanical and reduced to a standardized set of techniques applied in a predetermined sequence designed to extract information (Leurs 1997, 291). At the same time, it should be recognized that some issues are beyond the control of local people. One of the roles of RAP is to provide research results that will help the local people make structural changes and get resources from the outside. I will return to this issue in chapter 7, when I discuss bogus empowerment (see Team Leadership, p. 94; Bogus Empowerment, p. 140).

RAP can provide the research results local people need to get structural changes and resources from the outside.

Materials Collected in Advance

Assignments concerning the collection of documents in advance of the RAP should be made early and arrangements should include the reproduction and distribution of relevant materials to team members. Someone should be responsible for both collecting and cataloguing this material. If any of this material could be used in the final report, bibliographic information will be needed. Information collected in advance can have a major impact on methodology, even to the extent of showing that something else is needed instead of, or in addition to, a RAP. The information collected in advance will affect the initial guidelines used for semistructured interviews. When specific information is not available prior to the study, extra time and special techniques may be required to gather it (see Team Collection of Information, p. 27).

Local Team Members

Local team members, the insiders, should be identified as early in the process as possible. Basic information on RAP should be provided to them, and they should be included in the identification and collection of the advance materials. They must be present for orientations. Participation of local team members after they have been identified may depend upon whether they can be released from their normal activities, and ensuring this release should be a priority for the team leader (see Insiders/Outsiders, pp. 25, 89–94).

> **Full participation of the insider on the team will require their release from their regular duties.**

Orientation

Orientation on RAP methodology is critical, and sufficient time should be scheduled for it. If team members, including the insider, do not know each other, extra time is necessary for introductions and developing working relationships. If needed, information about the different team members should be distributed to all team members in advance of the orientation. Because of the importance of semistructured interviews for getting respondents to tell stories as opposed to just answering questions, the orientation may need to include practice interviewing, especially team interviewing. All team members need to understand that the purpose of the interview guidelines is to provide structure for discussions and that all of the questions do not have to be asked of the different respondents. If language interpreters are going to be used, it is critical that the team has experience with the use of the interpreters and that the interpreters understand the importance of reporting responses fully. The orientation should give as much attention to the iterative analysis/additional data collection process as to techniques for data collection. The orientation should include the use of the data display technique as part of the data analysis process, since this may be new to many team members (see Team Leadership, pp. 94–96; appendix C, Learning to RAP, p. 165).

Logistics—Keeping RAP from Becoming SAP

> **Attention to logistics helps keep RAP from becoming Slow Assessment Process (SAP).**

Logistics and scheduling are the two critical factors for preventing Rapid Assessment Process (RAP) from turning into Slow Assessment Process (SAP). If the RAP is to be rapid, the logistics must be in place and must function. The use overseas of computers and printers can be especially problematic. The voltage may be different, electrical plugs will not fit, versions of operating systems and application programs may be different, paper sizes are likely to be different, and there may be a need for software plug-ins to allow the printing of special characters. These problems can also be time-consuming at home.

If interviews are going to be recorded, someone should be responsible for testing the equipment and ensuring that batteries and blank tapes are available. Transcribing tapes and preparing research logs can be terribly time-consuming and a delay in transcribing tapes can delay the entire process. Problems with transcription of tapes during the community college RAP illustrate this. The college indicated that they would take responsibility and use students who needed the extra money. The understanding was that the maximum turnaround time on transcripts would be twenty-four hours. The RAP, however, was implemented during the exam period and by the end of the first twenty-four hours, only one of two tapes had been transcribed. Additional students who could transcribe the tapes were identified, and even regular support staff were reassigned to work on transcripts. With each day, there was a greater backlog of nontranscribed tapes. This intensified as the list of individuals to be interviewed grew significantly beyond what had been planned. Interviews were rescheduled in the hope that the transcripts of earlier interviews could be reviewed before new data were collected. Plans for team meetings to begin the data analysis process were also delayed. An already bad situation was made worse when two participants requested that someone from outside the organization transcribe their interviews. The team reluctantly decided to complete the draft report before the last three interviews were transcribed. The handwritten notes taken during these interviews were used to ensure that the input from the interviews was factored into the results.

Once the process had been delayed by even one day, individual team members began to have conflicts with other commitments. It then became increasingly difficult to get the entire team together. The ability to distribute transcripts to team members as e-mail attachments facilitated this process but made group work on the assignment of codes and the identification of themes for the later transcripts more difficult.

My experience has convinced me that (1) the team needs to have control over critical logistical issues such as tape transcription and (2) that having a person responsible for logistics is more important than having an additional academic discipline on the team (see Team Leadership, p. 94).

Schedule Flexibility

> ### Rapid does not mean rushed.

Rapid does not mean rushed. Schedules must be designed with sufficient flexibility that the team can take full advantage of unanticipated opportunities. Where a second appointment is scheduled soon after an earlier one, it may be useful to discuss flexibility with the second appointment and to have an agreed upon way of making contact. If you find yourself with a few minutes of unanticipated extra time, this time could be used for catching your breath or for performing some analysis as part of the iterative process before the next appointment.

> ### The number of interviews may have to be limited.

One of the most difficult aspects of scheduling is planning for the number of interviews to be conducted. This is further complicated if interviews are to be done at different sites and the number of sites has to be considered. One of the characteristics of qualitative research is that it is impossible to know in advance exactly how many interviews will be needed. Part of the planning process is estimating the number of interviews and then remaining flexible based on the information that is collected. If the first interviews reveal completely unanticipated issues and an extremely complex environment, there may be a need for more interviews. If redundancy in answers is evident early in the process, fewer interviews may be needed. A decision on the number of interviews should be a team decision. Consultation with the sponsors may also be necessary. These decisions should be explicit and recorded. Usually, the number of interviews should not be increased simply because additional individuals want to be interviewed.

The community college RAP illustrates some of the problems associated with trying to interview more individuals than needed. The initial number of individuals to be interviewed was not as fixed as it should have been. The general invitation to the members of the Student Services Division to meet with the team was made assuming it might be difficult to find individuals willing to take the time to be interviewed. The first several individuals interviewed were very enthusiastic about the process and quickly there was a list of individuals wanting to be interviewed that was much longer than the team had anticipated. By the end of the RAP at least 50 percent more interviews had been done than had been planned for, and there were still ten individuals who had not been interviewed but who wanted to participate. These additional interviews improved the richness of the data collected, but contributed very little to the identification of major themes. Redundancy in major themes was reached when about ten of the interviews had been conducted. In addition to the need to schedule the additional interviews, the desire to have transcripts of the interviews before reaching closure on the first draft report would have significantly delayed the process regardless of whether there had been a problem getting the tapes transcribed.

For this particular RAP, a better approach for scheduling would have been to (1) begin with a target number of interviews, (2) use more purposeful selection of the initial individuals to be interviewed, (3) interview others who wanted to participate on a first-come basis up to the target number of interviews, and (4) review and where appropriate revise the target number based on the results. Because each RAP is unique, the particular approach should be appropriate to the specific situation.

While Collecting Data

Interview Notes in Addition to Recording

Even the best tape recorder will miss things that a good note taker will catch. It may be issues of context or expression, or a specific and possibly important word. Tape recorders fail to pick up words, or even entire sentences, or may fail all together. The MEMOS made by a note taker also can jump-start the analysis process. As noted above, the availability of the handwritten notes on the interviews during the community college RAP allowed the data analysis process to proceed even when there was a delay in the completion of transcripts of the tapes (see Use of a Tape Recorder, p. 41).

> **Tape recorders should be expected to fail.**

The Twenty-Four-Hour Rule

The twenty-four-hour rule is that research logs should be prepared within twenty-four hours of the observations. This means that recorded interviews should be transcribed and field notes typed within twenty-four hours. The resulting research logs also need to be reviewed, even if only casually, before the next cycle of data collection starts. The twenty-four-hour rule is often impossible to follow, but still it's important to try. Even traditional ethnographers who work alone note the importance of the preparation of the log within twenty-four hours to prevent the failure to capture, or to capture accurately, interviews and observations that were missed in the field notes or the interview transcript. For RAP, the twenty-four-hour rule is critical because of the need to explicitly consider the results of a day of data collection before beginning the next round (see Field Notes and Logs, p. 54).

Changing the Role of Individual Team Members

Each team develops a unique dynamic, and various personalities are capable of a wide range of contributions to a team. The entire team should be asked to help ensure that no one is dominating and no one is being left out. It has been my experience that, even without explicit assignments, informal roles quickly develop. In some cases it may be desirable to encourage members to trade roles. If a team member is not able to function as part of the team, and especially if the behavior of that individual harms the teamwork of the other members, a hard and quick decision may be required to either sideline the individual or terminate the individual's participation. Ensuring dynamic team interaction and making the most of each individual's strengths are some of the most important responsibilities shared by the team leader and the entire team (see Team Dynamics, p. 83).

Follow-up Interviews with the Same Person

Traditional ethnographers who spend prolonged time in the field naturally return to the same individual numerous times. This is especially true of key informants who are able to discuss issues beyond their own experience.

The iterative process of data collection and analysis helps to focus each subsequent meeting. The time constraints of RAP may make follow-up interviews with the same person appear a luxury. My experience has been that such interviews are extremely productive and sometimes may be more useful than an interview with a new person (see Selection of Respondents, p. 45).

Follow-up interviews with the same person can sometimes be more useful than interviews with new respondents.

Spending Time at the Site

Eating and, when appropriate, sleeping at the site where a RAP is being done provides opportunities for informal discussions, follow-up discussions on topics of interest, and an understanding of the context of situations that may not be available otherwise. What comes up in the evening, at night, and in the early morning may never come up in interviews during "office hours." Even if it is not possible to share meals, it may be possible to share coffee or tea. The possible inconvenience for your hosts must always be considered when making a decision to spend extra time at the site. Chambers (1996) notes the importance of having unplanned time to "walk and wander around."

While Analyzing Data

Data Displays

The RAP team should experiment with a variety of ways for keeping the data analysis process active from the beginning. Data displays can be useful and ensure that all team members are involved in the process. Flip charts with bold color markers can be effective and are easily transported if the team is on the move. Tables based on comparisons between different cases and drawings similar to rich pictures are good beginning points for data displays. Data displays should always be dated (see Data Display, p. 68).

Presentation as a Way of Checking Back with Informants

Good ethnography is made better by checking back with the people who have provided the information. RAP places a special requirement on checking as a part of the ongoing data analysis process. Presentation to the local community should be arranged at several points during the RAP and not just near the end. Early presentation, before the team becomes convinced of its findings, provides a real opportunity for input from the groups being investigated. Preparation for presentations also is a way of ensuring that the data analysis process is ongoing (see Checking Back with Informants, p. 63).

Completion of the Draft Report

The RAP team, working together, should finish the draft report before the team disbands, even if this means less time collecting data. The preparation of the report is a critical part of the intensive team effort at data analysis. It usually makes sense to assign individual responsibility for the drafts of specific sections of the report. The sharing of these drafts provides wonderful opportunities for a team approach to data analysis. Word processing programs that allow changes to be clearly marked or tracked and ways of sharing files such as the use of e-mail attachments provide for collaboration on drafts without all parties having to be physically present at the same time. It is possible for every team member to know what each other member has added or changed. Team members can check and comment on whether additional quotes support conclusions that have already been reached and whether new or revised conclusions are appropriate. All team members can have the opportunity to review and edit as many drafts of a document as may be necessary.

Delays by the team in completing the final report can defeat the purpose for doing rapid research and can have serious implications for individuals who are waiting for the results. As was the case for the community college RAP, delays in the completion of a RAP are not always disastrous. There were more than eight weeks between the last interview and the submission of the final report for the community college RAP. A wrap-up meeting was scheduled between the team and members of the Student Services Division immediately following the submission and distribution of the final report. By the time that meeting occurred the results were already widely known, the leadership of the division had already been able to secure resources to begin addressing some of the issues raised in the report, and a plan of action involving formation of teams to address the different constraints was already underway. All situations are unique and implementation problems are pervasive, so there is a need for flexibility concerning all aspects of RAP, including the appropriate amount of time for completion.

Time Off

Even the most compulsive team member needs some time off. Team members need time away from each other, especially from the compulsive members. Weekends need to be honored, unless they are needed for data collection. In this case, another day should be identified for some time off. Experience with rapid appraisal in rural areas at Khon Kaen University in Thailand suggests that more than five hours per day spent in semistructured interviewing sessions is exhausting to even the heartiest team members and makes subsequent interviews less productive. More than about five days of this kind of fieldwork without a break can also be counterproductive. (Grandstaff and Grandstaff 1987, 78).

Improving RAP Skills

Learning from Experience

Learning from experience while doing RAP is not automatic. Without explicit attention to lessons that can be learned, mistakes are likely to be repeated. Part of the ongoing data analysis process should be asking which techniques are working and which ones need to be modified. This same process should be done at the end of the RAP. A beginning question should always be whether RAP was the most appropriate research approach for the specific investigation. Specific questions should be asked about team membership and team interaction. A final question on the research method is how rapid is too rapid or not rapid enough for a particular RAP.

Either learn from experience or forever repeat the same mistakes.

Including Process as Well as Content in the Report

Most RAP reports focus on what was learned and may include some attention to the methods used. They do not usually reflect on process, such as who took part, what they did, or how they did it (Leurs 1997, 291). There are at least two reasons why reports should also focus on process. The consumer of the report needs information on the process to determine how much confidence to place in the results. Attention to process is also necessary for the team to ensure that the process is as rigorous as it should be and that important elements have not been ignored. The RAP sheet provides a beginning for a consideration of process, but is not adequate by itself.

Sharing Lessons about the Methodology

Human Organization: Journal of the Society for Applied Anthropology has provided an important forum for discussion of rapid research methods and has also published articles based on these methods. There are several Internet, computer-based forums for discussing rapid methods. The "QUALRS-L" listserver invites discussion of qualitative research methods in general, including discussions of rapid methods. To subscribe, send this message to listserv@uga.cc.uga.edu: subscribe qualrs-1 <your name>. Discussions of qualitative research, including rapid research methods, can be found on several web pages (see Society for Applied Anthropology, <http://www.sfaa.net>; the PRA discussion list based at the University of Guelph, <http://www.oac.uoguelph.ca/~pi/pdrc/discuss.html>; PARnet at Cornell University, <http://www.parnet.org>; Resource Centre for Participatory Learning and Action, <http://www.oneworld.org.iied/resource/>; and Participation Group at IDS, <http://www.ids.ac.uk/ids/particip>).

Sharing RAP Reports

Researchers who use RAP are encouraged to publish their results in appropriate discipline-based journals. A list of peer-reviewed journals that publish the results of rapid research methods is included in the section on Problems with Credibility, p. 109. Practitioners of RAP are also encouraged to send information about publications or copies of their reports as e-mail attachments to RAP@gonzaga.edu. Files should be saved as Adobe Acrobat .pdf or as Microsoft Word .rft. All reports will be available from the RAP Research homepage at <http://www.gonzaga.edu/RAP>. Reports can also be shared by sending them to PARnet (see above). (See also Problems with Credibility, p. 108.)

WHO BENEFITS, WHO PAYS, AND WHO CALLS THE TUNE

Main Points

1. A RAP involves (1) the RAP team, (2) the stakeholders, and (3) the sponsors; interaction between these groups is influenced by differences in power and self-interests.
2. Even when the groups are acting in good faith with each other, there can be problems.
3. Unequal power relationships both within the RAP team and between the RAP team and the local stakeholders can seriously threaten the process. Unequal power between the different groups involved in a RAP can limit the independence of the RAP team.
4. Researchers often promise to deliver more than is possible and sponsors often demand more than is reasonable.
5. RAP can help define issues from the perspective of local participants, including identifying special terms and definitions, but limited time and participant observation in RAP preclude the depth of understanding that long-term fieldwork can produce.
6. **Propriety** refers to using procedures that are ethical and fair to those involved and affected.
7. Getting **informed consent** is essential for fair treatment.
8. The time people spend responding to the questions of a RAP team is valuable and this should be recognized by the RAP team.
9. Researchers rarely set out to betray the people who are the subjects of their inquiry, yet local participants are sometimes betrayed and often feel betrayed.
10. Betrayal is most likely to occur when the research team promises a level of confidentiality that is not delivered and when the research discloses information that should not be made public.

11. Bogus empowerment promises but does not deliver the confidence, competence, freedom, and resources people need to act on their own judgment.
12. Authentic empowerment gives people control over outcomes so they can be responsible for their activities.
13. The Statement of Professional and Ethical Responsibilities of the Society for Applied Anthropology provides a summary of ethical issues that should be considered.

Unequal Power and Constraints on Independence

A RAP involves three groups of players: (1) the RAP team, (2) the stakeholders, and (3) the sponsors. The stakeholders can be thought of as the individuals in the local group who are most likely to be impacted by the results of the RAP or any activities resulting from the RAP. Stakeholders are those ultimately affected, either positively (beneficiaries) or negatively. Stakeholders include both winners and losers, and those involved or excluded from the decision-making process (Overseas Development Administration 1995). The stakeholders are insiders for a situation and an objective of a RAP is to get at their perspective or understanding of a situation. The individuals the RAP team collects information from are stakeholders, but are unlikely to be all of the stakeholders. To some extent, the individuals with whom the team interacts represent an opportunity sample of the stakeholders. The sponsors often provide the funding for the RAP, initiate the arrangements, and are the clients to whom the RAP team is responsible. Often the sponsors are also stakeholders, since the results may have an impact on them. There are also some situations in which the local stakeholders sponsor the RAP, and the RAP team works directly for and is responsible to the stakeholders. The boundaries between these groups are permeable and individuals can belong to several groups at the same time. The reason that the distinction between the groups is important is that interaction between the groups is influenced by differences in power and self-interests. Even when the groups are acting in good faith with each other, and my assumption is that this is almost always the case, there can be problems.

Unequal power relationships both within the RAP team and between the RAP team and the local stakeholders can seriously threaten the process. RAP requires intensive and frank interaction between team members. It also requires that local people are willing to share their concerns and categories with outsiders. Unequal power relationships can have the consequences of the less powerful concluding that their best strategy is to tell the more powerful what they think they want to hear (Leurs 1997, 292).

> The less powerful may conclude it is in their best interest to tell the more powerful what they think they want to hear.

Recognition of the unequal power between the different groups involved in a RAP can help all parties recognize the limits on the independence of the RAP team. The sponsors have the power to either engage or not engage the services of the team. The sponsors may explicitly identify topics they want covered or topics that are "off limits." Often the sponsors control the release of any report prepared by the team, and they may reserve the rights to edit the report. In some situations, the RAP team may claim authorship of the report submitted to the sponsors and the sponsors may use this report to prepare a report that is clearly their own. The ability of the sponsors to fund additional research can have a subtle, but powerful, impact on the results of the RAP. As the RAP team attempts to increase the "usefulness" of their report, the sponsors can have tremendous influence on the report, since they define usefulness.

> Unequal power can limit the independence of the RAP team.

RAP teams are generally ad hoc, with team members selected because of what they can bring to the team. It has been my experience that outside team members are often selected from institutions of higher education, the sponsoring organization, or organizations involved in similar activities as the sponsoring organization. Organizations may set requirements that have to be met before their employees can engage in research. These can range from requiring a review of the research design by a committee formed to ensure the protection of human subjects, to a claim on the ownership and control of work resulting from the participation of their employee on a team. RAP team members from higher education will be influenced by how their organizations define legitimate research and the pressure in higher education to publish results. The quest for promotion to higher academic ranks and for tenure place pressure on the individual to produce results that can be published in peer-reviewed journals. Peer-reviewed journals tend to place value on the role of theoretical/conceptual frameworks for the analysis of research and what research can contribute to theory. Usually these types of issues are of very little or no interest to local stakeholders or sponsoring organizations. Because of the continued emphases in higher education on individual work, as opposed to teamwork, team members from higher education may feel pressured to produce individual reports in addition to their contribution to the team effort.

The home organization of RAP team members can influence their independence.

The influence of the market on employees of private firms is easier to recognize than the more subtle influence of major donors to not-for-profit organizations or institutions of higher education. The religious affiliation of not-for-profit organizations and institutions of higher education may also influence the types of research their employees can undertake.

Constraints on the independence of the RAP team should be recognized and may need to be discussed at the outset with the local stakeholders. If these constraints have had a significant impact on the results, this should be referenced in the final report. Factors that have significantly limited the independence of the RAP team should be added to the RAP Sheet.

Promising More Than Can be Delivered

It is easy for researchers to promise to deliver more than is possible and for sponsors to demand more than is reasonable. In some cases, unrealistic expectations appear to develop spontaneously. These issues are intensified by the nature of RAP. Some practitioners of RAP have been uncritical of the approach and have failed to recognize its limitations. Chambers (1991) cautions about overselling rapid research methods and suggests this provides grounds for discrediting these methods.

> **The RAP team should be careful not to promise more than it can deliver.**

RAP has been identified as an appropriate approach for inquiry when there is a need to get at the insiders' perspectives. Specific techniques for RAP are selected from qualitative research techniques that have proven effective in getting at the emic understanding of local situations. It must, however, be recognized that the time constraints on RAP and a limited role for participant observation preclude the depth of understanding that long-term field work is capable of producing. In many situations, carefully done RAP can be expected to produce more of an insider's perspective than alternatives such as questionnaire research and can be expected to produce emic understanding on a very limited number of issues. It is not unreasonable to expect RAP to help define issues from the perspective of local participants, to provide special terms and definitions as used locally, and to identify priorities based on local criteria. Even more than traditional qualitative research, RAP can produce results that appear to be superficial. Wolcott's comments about traditional qualitative research also would appear to apply to RAP: "Tighter conceptualization, cautious labeling, and a careful paper trail still seem the best protection against the inevitable charge that certain aspects of our work are superficial" (1995, 128).

In some of these situations, the RAP team has relatively more power in defining what are appropriate expectations than does the sponsor, because the team has relatively more information on the approach. I strongly believe the team has a responsibility to clearly identify the limits of RAP.

Of growing concern to many practitioners are the requests from sponsors to use rapid research methods in inappropriate situations. As noted earlier at several points, RAP is usually not appropriate when estimates of numbers or percentages are required. Also, as noted earlier, there are social/cultural situations in which team-based research will be inappropriate. There may be times when the power of the sponsor to provide the funding has to be countered with the power of the RAP team to provide information about the limits of the research approach. If information is not sufficient to change the views of the sponsors, it becomes the responsibility of the team to refuse to try to implement RAP where it would be inappropriate.

Who Benefits?

The assumption is that social science research is done to benefit the stakeholders, either directly or indirectly, through the production of knowledge that will in some way have a positive impact. RAP is even more closely tied to the assumption of providing benefits to stakeholders than is traditional research. However, RAP, like traditional research, often provides benefits not just to the local stakeholders but to the researchers, the sponsors, and the academic community.

> RAP benefits the team, the sponsors, and the academic community as well as the local community.

The RAP Team

I know of no full-time RAP team participants. Everyone I know of who has participated on a RAP team has described it as hard work, yet I have not heard any former participants indicate they would not like the opportunity to participate on another team. The question is what motivates individuals to take on this task. The factor that I have heard mentioned most frequently is the intrinsic rewards from working with others and providing assistance. Participation on a RAP team often provides a welcome break from regular activities and, in some cases, an opportunity to travel. Participation may provide monetary compensation, but I have yet to hear of participants for whom this was the motivating factor. For many individuals, both inside and outside of academia, there are rewards for doing research and completing reports or papers based on the research. Graduate students are uniquely well positioned to benefit from participation on a RAP team, since they can experiment with data collection and data analysis techniques that they may use in their own research. They also have the opportunity to develop expertise on new topics. As Wolcott writes, "Best intentions notwithstanding, I think we must concede that the person who stands to gain the most from any research is the researcher" (1995, 136).

The Sponsors

While a successful intervention resulting from a RAP may provide direct benefits to the local stakeholders, it can also provide significant benefits to the sponsors. Often, rapid research methods are initiated at higher levels of the bureaucracy to better understand problems, design new activities, or monitor ongoing activities of administrative units at lower levels of the organizations. Success in the lower administrative units or the local community may translate into increased resources for the sponsors. It should be assumed that sponsors are especially sensitive to the political context of research and that these considerations may impact decisions about what research is done, who does it, and how the results are disseminated.

The Academic Community

Organizations can benefit from learning about successes and failures in other organizations. Likewise, research approaches such as RAP can be improved by knowing about factors that contribute to the success or failure of specific inquiries. This type of information must be collected and disseminated. Traditionally, the results of research are included in reports or published in journal articles. Reports issued by organizations often have limited distribution, and other organizations that could make use of the results have no way of knowing they exist. Material published in academic journals may reach researchers who participate in RAP teams, but are less likely to reach local organizations. The RAP team has a responsibility to ensure that both the sponsors and the stakeholders understand the importance of disseminating the results of the RAP. This may require explicit agreement on confidentiality and an appreciation of the need to change details in the report to conceal the identity of the research site. The RAP team also has a responsibility to seek nontraditional ways of disseminating the results of their work, including but not limited to the use of the Internet. Purposeful selection of one or more RAP team members from organizations similar to the one being studied is one way of sharing information between organizations.

The Local Stakeholders

Often, the explicit objective of a RAP is to better define local issues in order to provide necessary external resources or change structural or policy constraints. One of the reasons that RAP needs credibility with the world beyond the local situation is to facilitate this process. While the power of outsiders over the local situation should be recognized, there is a danger that the role of the insiders in seeking solutions to their own problems can be ignored. Outside researchers can perpetuate a model of dependency. Even the research process can leave local people feeling that they have no voice in the identification of their problems or in suggesting solutions. With sensitivity to this issue and with the role of the insider as a full member of the RAP team, the RAP process can be a collaborative process of defining issues. The RAP activity can contribute to the development of local skills and systems for addressing issues that will be active after the RAP is finished. To be truly helpful to the insiders, the RAP process must help empower the local individuals while also helping them make their case for changes that can only be provided from the outside.

Possible Costs to Local Stakeholders

Propriety and Informed Consent

> ### Written informed consent is necessary.

Propriety refers to using procedures that are ethical and fair to those who are involved and are affected by the results of the assessment. I believe that getting informed consent is essential for the fair treatment of the local stakeholders. Some researchers have argued that interviews do not require written informed consent. I believe, along with most universities and funding agencies, that written informed consent is needed for interviews. Getting informed consent from participants provides an opportunity to discuss with them the purpose of the activity and to ensure that a minimum amount of agreement exists. The definition of informed consent can be expected to be culturally specific and this topic should be discussed with local key informants early in the process. When dealing with individuals who are functionally illiterate or who do not want to sign a form, one option is to have them record their consent. The form should be read to them and they should be asked to say either "yes" or "no" to indicate they agree with the terms. This should be played back to the respondent before the interview proceeds (and can be part of the testing of the recording equipment). Schoolchildren, other minors, and individuals with guardians require the formal, informed consent of their parents or legal guardians. Informed consent is premised on the individual having the freedom to decline without fear of retribution, a condition that individuals in institutions like prisons or even schools may not feel they have. Figure 7.1 is a sample informed consent form that can be adapted for specific situations. Universities and funding agencies may have their own forms that must be used.

Value of Time

The time people spend responding to the questions of a RAP team is valuable and the team should recognize this. One way to recognize the value of someone's time is to arrange meetings when it suits them. Recognizing and appreciating the value of someone's time is not the same as paying people to be interviewed. Generally, payment is to be avoided.

Betrayal

Researchers rarely set out to betray the people who are the subjects of their inquiry, yet local participants are sometimes betrayed and often feel betrayed. Miles and Huberman suggest that research can be considered an act of betrayal since "you make the private public and leave the locals to take the consequences" (Miles and Huberman 1994, 265). Betrayal is most likely to occur when the research team promises a level of confidentiality that is not delivered and when the research discloses information that should not be made public.

> **Betrayal occurs when promised confidentiality is not delivered.**

The process of providing informed consent to participate in research may include agreement that confidentiality will be provided. There are two

RAP Informed Consent Form

Researcher
Name: _____

Address: _____

Thank you for agreeing to participate in this Rapid Assessment Process (RAP). This form outlines the purposes of the study and provides a description of your involvement and rights.

The purpose of this activity is to get your opinions, insights, and suggestions about:

_____

_____

You are encouraged to ask questions at any time about the study and the methods we are using. Your suggestions and concerns are important to us.

We will use the information from this study to write a report. The report will be a public document.

Unless you are asked to sign a separate statement at the bottom of this form, your real name will not be used at any point in the written report. Instead, you and any other person and place you name will be given fictitious names (pseudonyms) that will be used in all verbal and written records and reports.

Audiotapes of interviews will be used only for this study and will not be played for any reasons other than to do this study.

Your participation in this study is voluntary. You have the right to withdraw at any point of the study, for any reason. If you withdraw, information collected from you and records and reports based on information you have provided will not be used.

Do you agree with the terms of this agreement?_____ (please write in **YES** or **NO**)

Your name (printed)_____

Your signature _____ The date_____
===
Special Consent to Use My Real Name

There may be special circumstances in which the use of your real name is desirable, such as the need to add credibility to statements or indicate support for proposed actions suggested by the community. If there is a possibility that your real name will be used, you will be asked to sign below. If your real name is used, you will be given the opportunity of reviewing the draft report and suggesting changes before it is finalized.

Do you grant permission for the use of your real name? _____(please write in YES or NO)

Your signature _____ The date_____

Figure 7.1. Sample Informed Consent Form

problems with promises of confidentiality. First, there may be significant cultural differences in how confidentiality is defined. This is likely to be more of a problem in the types of situations where RAP is needed than in other research situations. An informed consent form can have a very different meaning depending upon whether the reader is the researcher or the researched. Even when there is agreement on the meaning of a concept like confidentiality, there is very real danger to the participant if the researcher is naïve and falsely believes that it is possible to guarantee confidentiality. Accidental disclosure or forced disclosure by legal authorities can threaten confidentiality. An often overlooked source for accidental disclosure is the individuals who transcribe the interview tapes. This is especially true with individuals for whom transcribing tapes is not their primary responsibility. Concern about this issue by several of the participants in the community college RAP resulted in the requirements that some of the interview tapes be transcribed by individuals not associated with the college and that those involved in the transcription process sign a nondisclosure form. Figure 7.2 is a sample transcriber nondisclosure form that can be adapted to local conditions.

The RAP team is cautioned to let the participants in the inquiry understand that the team cannot guarantee confidentiality, but that they are committed to making a good faith effort if the participants desire confidentiality. Never promise more confidentiality than you can deliver.

The second situation in which betrayal may occur is when the results are reported. I fully agree with Wolcott that "no fieldworker ever has a license to tell all" (1995, 149). Wolcott suggests that an indication of the success of fieldwork is learning things that you did not want to learn and then facing decisions about what to disclose, "at what cost, for what audiences."

> I think fieldworkers should always have in mind clear boundaries for their inquiries. . . . You have to respect people's efforts to convey what *they* want you to hear, just as you hope they will talk candidly about what *you* want to hear. Your sense of courtesy will guide the extent to which you allow them just to "go on." The limits set for the inquiry should guide the extent of extraneous materials to record. (150)

Betrayal occurs when researchers incorrectly believe they have a license to tell all.

Rapid Assessment Process—RAP
Transcript Confidentiality Agreement

Thank you for agreeing to transcribe tapes of interviews for the Rapid Assessment Process (RAP). This form outlines the purpose of the study and provides a description of expectations about your involvement.

The purpose of this activity is to get participant's opinions, insights, and suggestions about_____

_____

_____

We have promised the participants that their real names (and the real names of anyone they refer to) will not be used at any point in the final written report, unless we have their written approval to use their real names. All participants will be given fictitious names (pseudonyms) that will be used in all verbal and written records and reports. We have also promised them that audiotapes of interviews will be used only for this study and will not be played for any reasons other than to do this study.

The ability of the team to accurately convey the statement of the participants depends to a large extent on your ability to accurately transcribe the tapes. If you have any questions about what is being said, please indicate it in the transcript by typing ??? (three question marks).

In agreeing to transcribe the interviews, you agree not to reveal their contents or even the names of the individuals interviewed.

Do you agree with the terms of this agreement? _____
(Please write in **YES** or **NO**)

Your name (printed)_____

Your signature _____ Date _____

Figure 7.2 Sample Transcriber Nondisclosure Form

Bogus Empowerment

The history of the Student Services Division at the community college had produced a culture characterized by mistrust. Experience had taught that little should be expected from efforts like the RAP. In this case, the ability of the participants to trust the RAP team depended to some extent upon their ability to trust the new dean. The new dean, however, hoped that the RAP process could help build some of the trust that was needed. The situation called for complete honesty about motives and processes involved in requesting the RAP team. The first meeting with the leadership team of the division provided the opportunity for the needed honesty. Without this honesty, the results could have been what Ciulla (1998) calls "bogus empowerment."

Ciulla contrasts bogus empowerment with authentic empowerment based on "a distinct set of moral understandings and commitments between leaders and followers, all based on honesty" (Ciulla 1998, 64). She notes that "empowerment is about giving people the confidence, competence, freedom, and resources to act on their own judgments" (63).

Ciulla makes a convincing argument that empowerment in the workplace requires a commitment by leaders to protect employees' jobs and by implication the resources they need to do their jobs. She notes that "when leaders really empower people, they give them the responsibility that comes with that power. But this does not mean that with less power, leaders have less responsibility. . . . Empowerment programs that give employees responsibility without control are cruel and stressful. Authentic empowerment gives employees control over outcomes so that they can be responsible for their work" (1998, 82).

Two aspects of authentic empowerment are especially relevant to RAP. Both the RAP team and the administration responsible for bringing in the RAP team must keep their promises. "The best way to do this is to make promises that they can keep. When leaders empower employees, they need to be clear about the extent of that power and avoid the temptation of engaging in hyperbole about the democratic nature of the organization." For the community college RAP, both the team and the dean were careful to clearly indicate that, even though all voices would be listened to, not all recommendations could or would be acted upon. Both the team and the dean also indicated that some issues would be identified that were beyond the influence of the dean, but that where appropriate they would be included in the report.

> RAP can be a collaborator to bogus empowerment by encouraging people to falsely believe that their input will be acted upon.

The second aspect of authentic empowerment especially relevant to RAP is the need to "overthrow some of the aspects of niceness" (Ciulla 1998, 83). Ciulla observes that "the truth is not always pleasant" and concludes that "when you really empower people, you don't just empower them to agree with you" (68).

> When you really empower people, you don't just empower them to agree with you.

The agreement between the RAP team and the dean was that the RAP team would have editorial control over the report. This information was communicated to the employees in the division. The report included controversial issues and issues for which there were no easy or even likely answers. It was also communicated to the members of the division that the RAP team planned to use the data from the study for scholarly activities as well as for whatever use the college wished to make of them. Finally, agreement on confidentiality was made, redefined, and reaffirmed on numerous occasions.

General Ethical Concerns

This chapter has highlighted several issues that are particularly relevant to RAP. A consideration of all of the general ethical issues involved in doing RAP is beyond the scope of this book. I believe, however, that the "Statement of Professional and Ethical Responsibilities" of the Society for Applied Anthropology provides a useful summary of issues that should be considered. This statement is reproduced in figure 7.3. Practitioners of RAP are reminded of the statement of Mirvis and Seashore (1982, 100 as cited in Miles and Huberman 1994), "Naiveté [about ethics] itself is unethical."

In chapter 8, we will consider the future of RAP by briefly examining its history and relationship to selected other research methodologies. The focus will be on what RAP shares with some of the other approaches, as opposed to differentiating RAP from them. RAP is flexible enough that it can be made more relevant to specific circumstances by borrowing from other approaches.

Additional Reading

Punch's (1986) book introduces issues of ethics in fieldwork within the context of politics. Chapter 11, Ethical Issues in Analysis, in Miles and Huberman (1994), is a comprehensive review of issues. Chapter 6,

Society for Applied Anthropology

This statement is a guide to professional behavior for the members of the Society for Applied Anthropology. As members or fellows of the society, we shall act in ways consistent with the responsibilities stated below irrespective of the specific circumstances of our employment.

1. To the peoples we study we owe disclosure of our research goals, methods, and sponsorship. The participation of people in our research activities shall only be on a voluntary basis. We shall provide a means through our research activities and in subsequent publications to maintain the confidentiality of those we study. The people we study must be made aware of the likely limits of confidentiality and must not be promised a greater degree of confidentiality than can be realistically expected under current legal circumstances in our respective nations. We shall, within the limits of our knowledge, disclose any significant risks to those we study that may result from our activities.

2. To the communities ultimately affected by our activities we owe our respect for their dignity, integrity, and worth. We recognize that human survival is contingent upon the continued existence of a diversity of human communities, and guide our professional activities accordingly. We will avoid taking or recommending action on behalf of a sponsor which is harmful to the interests of the community.

3. To our social colleagues we have the responsibility to not engage in actions that impede their reasonable professional activities. Among other things, this means that, while respecting the needs, responsibilities, and legitimate proprietary interests of our sponsors we should not impede the flow of information about research outcomes and professional practice techniques. We shall accurately report the contributions of colleagues to our work. We shall not condone falsification or distortion by others. We should not prejudice communities or agencies against a colleague for reasons of personal gain.

4. To our students, interns, or trainees, we owe nondiscriminatory access to our training services. We shall provide training which is informed, accurate, and relevant to the needs of the larger society. We recognize the need for continuing education so as to maintain our skill and knowledge at a high level. Our training should inform students as to their ethical responsibilities. Student contributions to our professional activities, including both research and publication, should be adequately recognized.

5. To our employers and other sponsors we owe accurate reporting of our qualifications and competent, efficient, and timely performance of the work we undertake for them. We shall establish a clear understanding with each employer or other sponsor as to the nature of our professional responsibilities. We shall report our research and other activities accurately. We have the obligation to attempt to prevent distortion or suppression of research results or policy recommendations by concerned agencies.

6. To society as a whole we owe the benefit of our special knowledge and skills in interpreting sociocultural systems. We should communicate our understanding of human life to the society at large.

Figure 7.3. Statement of Professional and Ethical Responsibilities

Fieldwork: The Darker Arts, in Wolcott (1995), raises important issues that I have not seen covered elsewhere. Ciulla (1998) provides a label for something many of us have experienced and all of us wish to avoid doing to others: bogus empowerment.

Ciulla, J. B. 1998. Leadership and the problem of bogus empowerment. In *Ethics: The heart of leadership*, ed. J. B. Ciulla, 63–86. Westport, Conn.: Quorum Books.

Miles, M. B., and A. M. Huberman. 1994. *Qualitative data analysis: An expanded sourcebook*. 2d ed. Thousands Oaks, Calif.: Sage.

Punch, M. 1986. *The politics and ethics of fieldwork*. Beverly Hills, Calif.: Sage.

Wolcott, H. F. 1995. *The art of fieldwork*. Walnut Creek, Calif.: AltaMira.

THE RAP FAMILY TREE

Main Points

1. RAP has its roots in farming systems research.
2. RAP is a direct descendant of Rapid Appraisal, Rapid Assessment, and Rapid Rural Appraisal.
3. Not everything referred to as "Rapid Appraisal" or "Rapid Assessment" meets the methodological requirements of RAP.
4. RAP represents a middle ground that is far more participatory than early versions of Rapid Appraisal, but not necessarily as participatory as **Participatory Appraisal (PRA)**.
5. Appreciative Inquiry focuses on identifying what is going well, and RAP can greatly benefit from an Appreciative Inquiry approach, but does not require it.
6. Despite their different origins, many rapid research methods have in common the fact that they were introduced to address the need for cost-effective and timely results in rapidly changing situations.
7. Most of the rapid research methods can be described as "first-cut assessments of . . . poorly known areas" and as "organized common sense, freed from the chains of inappropriate professionalism."
8. RAP shares characteristics with Rapid Guided Survey, cultural scenes, micro-ethnography, and quick ethnography.
9. The common thread in the evolution of rapid research methods is the conclusion that the world was moving too quickly for the normal, disciplinary approaches.
10. RAP is an idea whose time has come.

Farming Systems Research and Rapid Research

RAP has its roots in the development of farming systems research in the late 1970s (see Shaner et al. 1982). Farming systems research was based on a consideration of people along with their plants and livestock. There was an increased need to know about the conditions farmers faced when they practiced agriculture and neither research tourism nor questionnaire survey research could provide solid and timely results. Photocopies of papers about new approaches for research made their way to projects around the world, including Sudan, where I was assigned at the time. I was especially impressed with a paper by Peter Hildebrand (1979) describing a research approach based on teamwork called "Sondeo." I then received copies of several other papers on rapid, team-based research from the 1979 workshop at the Institute of Development Studies, University of Sussex, including papers by Robert Chambers. The title of this workshop used the phrase "Rapid Rural Appraisal." This phrase and variants of it became associated with rapid, team-based research. Despite differences over details, there was a general consensus that Rapid Rural Appraisal was based on small multidisciplinary teams using semistructured interviews to collect information and that the entire process could be completed in one to six weeks.

RAP and Rapid Appraisal/Rapid Assessment

RAP is a direct descendant of Rapid Appraisal, Rapid Assessment, and Rapid Rural Appraisal. One of the strengths of the approach has always been its flexibility. The approach has continued to evolve and the terms associated with it have been used in different ways, to describe a wide range of activities. While I believe RAP can also be referred to as "Rapid Appraisal" or "Rapid Assessment," I do not believe that everything that is labeled with these terms would meet the methodological requirements of RAP.

RAP and Participatory Appraisal

Since the mid-1980s people in the international development community have increasingly emphasized "participatory" approaches. The advocates of Participatory Appraisal (PRA) would probably say that RAP is not "participatory." They might argue that RAP is closer to traditional rapid appraisal, with its focus on data collecting, analysis done mainly by outsiders, and dependence on observations and semistructured interviews. They would contrast this with PRA, with its focus on enabling local people to share, embrace, and analyze their knowledge of life and to plan and act based on mapping, diagramming, and comparison. For PRA the assumption is that local people will do almost all of the investigation and analysis and will then share with the outsiders (Chambers and Blackburn 1996). Advocates of PRA refer to "the use of local graphic representations created by the community that legitimize local knowledge and promote empowerment" (CASL 1999).

I would argue that RAP represents a middle ground that is far more participatory than early versions of Rapid Appraisal but not as participatory as PRA. There is local representation on the RAP team. RAP is based on data collection and analysis by the team, including the insider on the team. PRA makes extensive use of drawing and diagramming by the local community for both information collection and analysis. RAP identifies these as optional techniques to supplement semistructured interviewing and direct observation. RAP does not necessarily focus as much on empowering as does PRA. However, as discussed in chapter 7, RAP can and should empower local people. The differences in approaches are matters of degrees. The real difference is the audience. RAP is based on the assumption that local problems often reflect structural conditions over which local people have little or no control. The changes that are needed may require externally supported interventions, policy changes, or resources. Support for these types of changes requires research methodologies with credibility among the outsiders. RAP is designed to have this type of credibility. There are times when a RAP is more appropriate, times when a PRA is more appropriate, times when both are needed, and still other times when the most appropriate methodology is a combination of the two.

RAP and Participatory Poverty Assessments

Participatory Poverty Assessment, also called Participatory Policy Research, is based on directly presenting to policy makers the views of the poor as part of a national dialogue to influence policy. The assumption is that poor people can identify dimensions of poverty other than income and

147

consumption, those usually used in policy analysis. These additional issues might include vulnerability, isolation, security, self-respect, powerlessness, and dignity. The goal is better-informed policymakers. Participatory Policy Research purports to add to the methodology used by other rapid research methods a focus on local people's understanding of the problem and local people's capability to analyze policy impact (Robb 1999). RAP can contribute to Participatory Poverty Assessments a range of specific research techniques, explicit guidance on the use of teams (including both insiders and outsiders), and approaches for analyzing the results.

RAP and Appreciative Inquiry

Appreciative Inquiry focuses on identifying what is going well, determining the conditions that make excellence possible, and encouraging those conditions within the organizational culture. RAP can greatly benefit from an Appreciative Inquiry approach, but does not require it. Hammond and Hall (1998) describe Appreciative Inquiry as a way of thinking, seeing, and acting for purposeful change in organizations. They suggest that the focus for traditional organizational development consultants is looking for problems and that looking for problems ensures they are found and made bigger. Hammond and Hall contrast traditional organizational development with Appreciative Inquiry as in table 8.1.

Table 8.1 Traditional versus Appreciative Inquiry

TRADITIONAL	APPRECIATIVE INQUIRY
Define the problem	Search for solutions that already exist
Fix what's broken	Amplify what is working
Focus on decay	Focus on life-giving forces
What problems are you having?	What is working well around here?

The assumptions of Appreciative Inquiry are:

1. In every society, organization, or group, something works.

2. What we focus on becomes our reality.

3. Reality is created in the moment and there are multiple realities.

4. The act of asking questions of an organization or group influences the group in some way.

5. People have more confidence and comfort to journey to the future (the unknown) when they carry forward parts of the past (the known).

6. If we carry parts of the past forward, they should be what is best about the past.

7. It is important to value differences.

8. The language we use creates our reality (Hammond 1998, 21–22).

Appreciative Inquiry is based on engaging the entire system in a discussion of what works, with analysis focused on discovering "themes and dreams of 'what could be' and 'what will be'" (Hammond and Hall 1998). The future is "envisioned" through an analysis of the past and the best of the past is maintained and stretched into the future.

RAP can learn from and contribute to Participatory Appraisal, Participatory Poverty Assessment, and Appreciative Inquiry.

Other Rapid Research Methods

Beginning in the late 1970s various rapid research methods were developed almost simultaneously to investigate different problems encountered in developing countries. These methods appeared in agriculture, community development, rural development, marketing, and health care. Despite their different origins, these methods have in common the fact that they were introduced to address the need for cost-effective and timely results in rapidly changing situations. They also share many of the characteristics of an approach to qualitative research developed by anthropologists and referred to as ethnography.

The objective for most of the approaches that are identified as rapid research methods could be summarized as "first-cut assessments of . . . poorly known areas" (Conservation International 1991, 1). The element of compromise is explicit in statements that describe them as "a middle zone between . . . fairly quick and fairly clean" (Chambers 1991, 521). Rapid Appraisal was described as "organized common sense, freed from the chains of inappropriate professionalism" (Chambers 1980, 15) and "a form of appropriate technology: cheap, practical and fast" (Bradfield 1981 cited in Rhoades 1982, 5). These last two comments are especially relevant to RAP.

Rapid Guided Survey, Cultural Scenes, and Micro-Ethnography

In 1941, Robert Redfield and Sol Tax conducted a three-day field survey and used the term "Rapid Guided Survey" (Wolcott 1995, 109). Despite having a clear idea of the information they sought, since they were in the seventh year of their fieldwork, they attributed their success with the survey at least in part to sheer luck.

In the early 1970s Spradley and McCurdy (1972) presented an approach for teaching undergraduate students about ethnographic research by doing "cultural descriptions" of "cultural scenes." Their book covered ways of discovering cultural categories, organizing them into larger domains, and identifying the elements or attributes that give them meanings. They estimated that the total amount of time needed for the entire process was about the same time as it should take an undergraduate student to do a library research paper. They argued that "an adequate study can be done in a limited amount of time by restricting the scope of your investigation" (5). They also pointed out that even a researcher spending two years in the field can examine only a few topics in depth and also has to restrict his or her investigation. They suggested that the twelve ethnographic reports done by their students and included in their book "demonstrate the way cultural scenes in our own society can be studied" (ix).

In 1980 Spradley (30) suggested labels for various levels of ethnography. These labels included "macro-ethnography" for the study of a complex society and "micro-ethnography" for the study of a single social situation.

Quick Ethnography

Recently, Handwerker (2001) has introduced the term "Quick Ethnography" to describe an approach for doing "high quality" ethnographic research in between thirty and ninety days. His approach is based on starting with a clear vision of the goals of the research and paying close attention to how to achieve them. This focus is combined with techniques for making the best possible use of time in the field. Handwerker notes that this approach assumes the principal researcher is well trained in qualitative research and has sophisticated computer skills, including the use of quantitative and qualitative data analysis computer programs.

Rapid Ethnography as an Alternative Label for RAP

I considered using the phrase "Rapid Ethnography" instead of "Rapid Assessment Process" because ethnography accurately describes the methodology. Ethnography is based on data collected from documents, participant observation, and semistructured interviewing. Ethnography focuses on observable and learned patterns of behavior by a social group or individuals within the group. Ethnography is capable of generating a cultural portrait based on observations and listening to the voices of informants. All of the statements above apply to RAP as well as to ethnography (the overlap between ethnography and RAP was explored in the last half of chapter 2). For ethnographers like Wolcott (1995, 110) the problem is that "terms like *ethnography* or *fieldwork* join uneasily with a qualifier like *rapid*." Ethnography is usually defined as based on prolonged fieldwork (Bernard 1995; see Creswell 1998 for a summary). Wolcott (1995) explicitly equates ethnography with extended fieldwork (even reserving the term fieldwork for extensive fieldwork) and the production of monograph-length reports.

In 1995 Bernard suggested that it might be possible to achieve competency in another culture in as few as three months (151). Wolcott was skeptical and responded by saying "I hope Bernard has not inadvertently foreshortened the acceptable period for fieldwork for those who will carefully misread his statement or reassure themselves that the three months he says is adequate to *establish* oneself in the field is all the time one needs to devote to a study" (1995, 110). Wolcott suggests that when one is in doubt as to whether something is "genuine ethnography," one should select a more cautious term. Given near consensus that ethnography requires prolonged fieldwork, I chose the term "Rapid Assessment Process" instead of "Rapid Ethnography."

Rapid Research Methods in Different Fields

Figure 8.1 illustrates the wide range of topics that have been investigated using rapid research methods, the different groups and organiza-

Agriculture

Sondeo	(Hildebrand 1979)
Rapid Rural Appraisal	(Collinson 1979)
Rapid Reconnaissance	(Honadle 1982)
Exploratory Survey	(Collinson 1981)
Informal Methods	(Shaner et al. 1982)
Reconnaissance Survey	(Shaner et al. 1982)
Informal Agricultural Survey	(Rhoades 1982)
Farming Systems Research	(Brush 1986)
Rapid Rural Appraisal	(Abalu et al. 1987)
Rapid Rural Appraisal	(Khon Kaen University 1987)
Rapid Rural Appraisal	(McCracken 1988)
Diagnostic Case Study	(Doorman 1990)

Community and Rural Development

Rapid Rural Appraisal	(Chambers 1979)
Participatory Rural Appraisal	(CUNES 1989)
Participatory Rural Appraisal	(Chambers 1991)
Rapid Ethnographic Appraisal (minority home ownership)	(Ratner 1996)
Rapid Appraisal Techniques in Social Work	(Aigbe 1996)
Rapid Appraisal	(Campa and Skartvedt 1997)
Rapid City-Wide Needs Assessment	(Ervin 1997)
Incorporating Local History	(Astone 1998)
Rapid Rural Appraisal (rural water supply)	(Salamon et al. 1998)
Participatory Rural Communication Appraisal	(Van der Stichele 1998)

Conservation and Natural Resources

Rapid Assessment Program (RAP)	(Conservation International 1991)
Environmental Rapid Assessments	(Abate 1992)
Rapid Appraisal (wildlife presence)	(Matzke 1995)
Rapid Rural Appraisal (coastal resource planning)	(Pido 1995)
Participatory Rural Appraisal (aquaculture)	(Townsley 1996)
Rapid Assessment Program (RAP)	(NOAA's Damage Assessment and Restoration Staff 1997)
Wetland Rapid Assessment Procedure (WRAP)	(South Florida Water Management District 1997)
Rapid Assessment Protocol (RAP) (reef assessment)	(Ginsburg et al. 1998)

Health and Family Planning

Rapid Assessment Procedure (RAP)	(Scrimshaw and Gleason 1992)
Rapid Assessment of Nutrition and Primary Health Care	(Scrimshaw 1992)

Figure 8.1. Examples of Rapid Research from Different Fields

Rapid Epidemiological Assessment (REA)	(Vlassoff and Tanner 1992)
Rapid Assessment Procedures (RAP) (household management of diarrhea)	(Herman and Bentley 1993)
Rapid Rural Appraisal (epidemiology)	(Henderson 1995)
Rapid Appraisal	(Dale and Shipman 1996)
Rapid Rural Appraisal (health planning)	(Rifkin 1996)
Focused Ethnographic Study (FES)	(Pelto and Glove, as cited in UNFPA 1997)
Rapid Anthropological Assessment Procedures (RAAP)	(UNFPA 1997)
Rapid Assessment Procedures (RAP) (women's health)	(Gittelsohn et al. 1998)
Rapid Anthropological Assessment	(Manderson 1998)
Rapid Assessment and Responses Guide on Substance Use and Sexual Risk (SEX-RAR)	(Rhodes and Stimson 1998)
Rapid Appraisal (health needs)	(Murray 1999)

Marketing

Commodity Systems Assessment Methodology (CSAM)	(la Gra 1990)
Rapid Marketing Appraisal (RMA)	(Menegay et al. 1990)
Market Information Needs Assessment (MINA)	(Guyton 1992)
Development Market Research (DMR)	(Epstein 1992)

Miscellaneous and General

Rapid Anthropological Procedure (RAP)	(Kumar 1987)
Rapid and Reliable Research Methods	(Van Willigen and Finan 1991)
Rapid Evaluation Methodology (REM)	(Anker et al. 1993)
Rapid Rural Appraisal	(Dunn 1994)
Rapid Rural Appraisal (village information needs)	(Sturges and Chimseu 1996)
Rapid Ethnographic Assessment (commemorative event planning)	(Van Horn et al. 1996)
Rapid Ethnographic Assessment (park users)	(Williams and Ramos 1997)
Rapid Assessment Protocol (RAP)	(Ginsburg et al. 1998)

Figure 8.1. *(continued)*

tions that have used these methods, and the extent to which methods have been adapted to meet different needs. While most of these examples report on specific research completed using rapid methods, a few are general articles about rapid research methods that make reference to specific studies. All of the examples are from applied situations in which rapid research was used to respond to the need for timely and cost-effective results. Not all of the examples meet the minimum requirements of RAP as outlined in this book. The list is not meant to be a bibliography of rapid research methods. General bibliographies include *Rapid Rural Appraisal: Annotated Bibliography* (Hassin-Brack 1988) and the *Annotated Bibliography on Gender, Rapid Rural Appraisal and Participatory Rural Appraisal* (BRIDGES 1994). The list is designed to provide an illustration of some of the ways rapid research methods have been used. I am certain that there are others and that more are being named all the time.

The examples are organized by broad fields and by year of publication. In some cases it was difficult to decide on the most appropriate field.

The Future of RAP and Concluding Comments

The accelerating rate of change in the world and a lessening of financial support for long-term research have driven the increasing interest in rapid research methods. According to Scrimshaw, "If you look back at how RAP evolved, the common thread is people reached the conclusion that the world was moving too quickly for the normal, disciplinary approaches" (Abate 1992, 486). As early as 1992, Scrimshaw said "RAP is an idea whose time has come" (Abate 1992, 486). There is a growing consensus among researchers and practitioners in a number of fields that rapid research methods are here to stay. I firmly believe that RAP is relevant to a wide range of situations in which a qualitative approach to inquiry is needed, but either limited time or limited resources preclude traditional, long-term fieldwork. The challenge will be to embrace the potential of RAP, while at the same time recognizing its limitations. It is my hope that this book will contribute to the process.

RAP is an idea whose time has come.

Additional Reading

Excellent materials on participation are available from the Institute of Development Studies (1996) and at their web site, <http://www.ids.susx.ac.

uk/ids/partricip/research.html>. Other web sites dealing with participation include the USAID's *Internet Guide for Participation,* <http://www.usaid.gov/about/part_devel/docs/webguide.htm> (USAID 2000), and the Community Economic Development Centre at Simon Fraser University's *Annotated Bibliography: Readings in Research Methods in Community Economic Development,* section on "Participatory Action Research," <http://virtual-u.ssfu.ca/cedc/forestcomm/pprworking/ABsmith.htm> (Smith 2000). The Appreciative Inquiry Resource List, <http://www.serve.com/taos/appreciative.html> (Dole and Cooperrider 2000), identifies more than seventy-five publications on Appreciative Inquiry. The full text of Scrimshaw and Gleason (1992), Gittelsohn et al. (1998), Herman and Bentley (1993), and numerous other publications about rapid research methods in the health and nutrition field are available on-line and free through the United Nations University <http://www.who.int/substance_abuse/pages.docs.html>. Many of the web sites referred to in this book can be expected to change or even disappear. The status of these sites, along with corrections and new sites, can be found at <http://www.gonzaga.edu/RAP>.

CASL (Community Adaptation and Sustainable Livelihoods). 1999. *Participatory research for sustainable livelihoods: A guide for field projects on adaptive strategies: Participatory Rural Appraisal (PRA).* Retrieved July 6, 2000, from <http://iisd1.iisd.ca/casl/CASLGuide/PRA.htm>.

Hammond, S. A. 1998. *The thin book of appreciative inquiry.* 2d ed. Plano, Tex.: Thin Books.

Holland, J., and J. Blackburn. 1998. *Whose voice? Participatory research and policy change.* Brighton, England: Institute of Development Studies.

Robb, C. M. 1999. *Can the poor influence policy? Participatory Poverty Assessments in the developing world.* Washington, D.C.: World Bank.

APPENDIX A. EXECUTIVE SUMMARY, COMMUNITY COLLEGE RAP

Summary of the Results
Building upon Strengths and Overcoming Constraints to Improve Student Services at a Community College: Report of a Rapid Assessment Process (RAP)

March 17, 2000
James Beebe, Dale Abendroth, Nancy Chase, and Grace Leaf

Most of the comments of the participants were grouped into categories and identified as *constraints* to the ability of the people involved in the Student Services Division to do the best job possible. There was general consensus that performance was not always as good as it should have been, that most people truly wanted to do better, but that there were a range of interrelated factors that prevented this from happening. The six constraints were (a) communication, (b) physical space, (c) technology, (d) utilization of people's time, talents, and creativity, (e) increases in the number and complexity of regulations, and (f) inadequate resources.

Communication

Virtually all of the interviews included references to problems with communication. Communication was seen as a problem at all levels, individual to individual, individual to supervisor, individual to administration, department to department, department to administration, and division to division. The need for open and consistent communication was expressed by many individuals. One of the most insightful comments on inadequate communications was voiced by a participant who said "It's just quietness and you just start to wonder what's going on when it's so quiet."

Physical Space

Physical space was another theme that emerged as a constraint to people in doing the best job possible. Individuals expressed frustration at having to work in crowded, unattractive areas that afforded little privacy. A strong case was made by several participants for private offices as opposed to cubicles. "I think we need individual offices and not cubicles for the confidentiality that we have to work with. Even though I have a cubicle, you can hear everything. Students don't want to talk about their life when other people can hear."

Technology

There was a rather widespread conviction that technology, rather than reducing work or making the existing work easier, had merely added "insult to injury." Technology was seen as creating additional work and further complicating an already complicated environment. It was viewed as simply another load on employees and as a seriously limiting factor for many individuals. There was also a concern that the use of technology reduced personal contact with students. There was a widespread perception that many students were better prepared for technology than some of those within the Student Services Division. The students interviewed by the RAP team reported that they did not have a problem with technology, but often did have a problem with the way the community college implemented it.

Utilization of People's Time, Talents, and Creativity

Several members of the community referred to the tremendous enthusiasm, talents, creativity, and motivation of people with whom they work. Often these comments were in the context of "There is a lot of creativity that is stifled here." One participant was emphatic that "the only way we're going to really compete and be a dynamic institution is to recognize every staff person, every faculty person has a little leadership role."

Regulations

Numerous participants in this study commented upon the constraints imposed by regulations at the district, state, and federal levels. Comments were often in the context of increases in these regulations and often included a note of resignation. "We have to abide by federal regulations."

The need for some regulations was recognized. One participant noted that "we are a bureaucracy and if there wasn't some order to it, you know it would be total chaos, but sometimes it is difficult to get things to happen in as timely a fashion as you wish you could." There was a reluctant admission that there could sometimes be an advantage to the delays imposed by regulations.

Inadequate Resources

The general consensus was that resources for student services were declining. "I think in the time that I have been here, all I have ever seen is less money." A minority view was that overall resources were adequate but there was a problem with allocation. Many of these comments suggested that the administration was responsible for individual units getting less resources than they needed.

Staffing was the resource issue most often raised. Almost everyone commented on increased work levels, increased demands, reduced "downtime," and staff shortages.

Suggestions for dealing with inadequate resources, including staff, fell into three categories: (a) increase resources, (b) reallocate resources from one unit to another (usually from some other unit to "my" unit), and (c) use resources in better, more creative ways.

Facilitating Change

Specific suggestions for facilitating change emerged from the conversations about changes necessary for people to do the best job possible. The overarching theme was the need to develop trust. Trust was consistently linked to stability within the leadership team, open and consistent communication both vertically and horizontally, and developing a knowledge and appreciation of others' roles within student services. These themes were often interwoven in participant's conversation: "The more we know about each other, the more we trust each other, and if we trust each other, we'll be able to work with each other." Other suggestions to enhance the division's work included sharing information about successful approaches used other places and the creation of venues to discuss new ways of doing things.

Numerous participants were highly skeptical that the RAP, or any study, could have a significant impact on conditions in the division. Several participants indicated that it was their hope that the RAP could be a factor in improving communication and would thereby facilitate change. There was, however, recognition that some of the issues that must be addressed were fundamental and there would be no easy or quick solutions. Within this context there was caution about expecting too much from any specific activity and a call for increasing the "good faith" that most agreed needed to be expanded.

APPENDIX B. EXECUTIVE SUMMARY, POLISH STATE FARMS RAP

Management and Transformation to a Market Economy: A Rapid Appraisal of State Farms in the Koszalin Voivodship, Poland[1]

October 11, 1991

James Beebe, John Farrell, Kent Olson, and Terrie Kolodziej with Tomasz Adamczyk.

State farms in Poland occupy about 18 percent of the agricultural land, but are a significant part of the economy and employ approximately 500,000 workers. The goal of the government of Poland was to eventually privatize these farms. A significant number of state farms were failing before they could be privatized and changes in management were necessary to counter this trend.

During the two years before this study, directors of state farms had been confronted with severe problems resulting from the transformation of the Polish economy. For the first time directors had to deal with high inflation and interest rates, with prices that did not always cover production costs, and with a general lack of demand. This environment, complicated by unclear government agricultural policy, had brought into focus differences in the management skills of directors.

Radical economic transformation provided the context for a rapid appraisal of the management skills of state farm directors in Koszalin Voivodship. The purpose of this rapid appraisal was to assess management responses to the economic environment. The principle research method was semistructured interviews of individual respondents and groups. Information from more than 110 hours of interviews was combined with direct observations of ten state farms. The collection and analysis of the data was an iterative process.

Variability in the reactions of state farm directors ranged from no response to changes in organizational structure, crop and livestock production, financial management, levels of employment, and marketing. These responses were analyzed based on the directors' explanations of what had happened. These responses suggested that many state farm directors did not fully understand how a market operates. This lack of full understanding appeared to be the most serious in areas of (1) risk, (2) information, (3) production vs. profits, (4) price determination, and (5) financial management.

Risk. From their comments, it appeared that many state farm directors believed the government should provide an essentially risk-free environment. They did not recognize that in a market economy government can reduce risk but cannot eliminate it. They tended to view risk as always negative, and failed to recognize that risk may provide opportunities for increased profits and growth for more creative managers.

Information. Many directors apparently had failed to recognize the power of information to reduce risk. They did not use available information as efficiently as they could have as a planning tool.

Production vs. profit. For many directors of state farms, decisions were aimed at achieving production goals. It will take considerable effort to convince state farm directors, bankers, and others that, under some conditions, levels of inputs will have to be cut and that physical production will and should fall.

Price determination. Many directors were not ready to accept that, in a market economy, prices are the result of supply and demand. Some directors found it incomprehensible that the government would not establish prices to cover their costs of production. Directors need to understand that in a market there may be times when prices will not cover costs.

Financial management. Many directors did not understand that good financial management is crucial in a market environment. In the past, state farm directors had access to subsidized short-term credit. With the reduction of credit availability, cash-flow projections and the implications of cash flow for the timing of activities became the most critical financial management skill for many state farm directors.

There was general agreement that some of the most serious problems facing state farms cannot be resolved at the farm level. These included general agricultural policy, the monopoly position of farm output purchasers, bank policy, and the social role of state farms, especially the issue of apartments to the workers. The responses of the state farm directors, their understanding of how a market economy operates, and the problems that could not be resolved at the farm level led to three specific suggestions about changes in the advisory/extension services in Poland.

Focus on relative success. Because most directors appeared to recognize only a subset of the possible responses, the recommendation was that the advisory service disseminate information on the relatively more successful directors. The assumption was that this would help other directors recognize new options and convince them that success is possible.

Information. The second recommendation was that the agricultural advisory services identify specific information that directors and farmers want and the form in which it will be most useful and then make the information available.

Better understanding of the five issues related to a market economy. The third recommendation was that the advisory service help directors and others address the issues of risk, information, profits, price determination, and financial management by: (1) helping them locate and interpret market information necessary to predict a range of likely prices, (2) helping them adjust production decisions in response to this range of prices, and (3) helping them improve financial management, beginning with cash-flow analysis, in order to implement decisions based on price estimates.

An analysis of the situation faced by the directors of the state farms and the current role of the advisory services led to three specific suggestions for the advisory services: (1) Intensive training for members of the advisory services, the current directors of state farms, and future directors of these farms after privatization should be based on simulation, case studies, and the manipulation of "real-world" data (as opposed to classroom lectures). (2) The role of private sector Polish consultants should be encouraged and supported to complement the role of the public sector advisory service. (3) During the transformation process, the advisory service should assist in (a) valuing assets and dealing with legal issues, (b) identifying land that should not be in production and advising how to maintain and improve the quality of this land, and (c) promoting community development activities for unemployed state farm workers.

[1] Report prepared for the Extension Service of the United States Department of Agriculture (USDA) and the Polish Ministry of Agriculture and Food Economy under the Polish/American Extension Project.

APPENDIX C. LEARNING TO RAP

The experience of those who have used the approach suggests that RAP could be relevant to a much wider audience. For individuals who have had limited experience with qualitative techniques, there is a need to provide a strong rationale for and an introduction to qualitative research. For individuals with a background in qualitative research, there is a need to help them understand ways in which RAP differs from traditional approaches. There is general consensus from users that RAP is best learned while participating as a team member with someone with experience, but that, since rapid research methods are "organized common sense," they can be self-taught. Since learning to listen while discussing issues with people is so critical for RAP, everyone should have the opportunity of doing a videotaped semistructured interview. Just watching the results can have a significant impact on the time one gives for others to respond before talking again. From reading reports by others, one can learn a significant amount about the methodology and what are realistic expectations of it. A final recommendation for acquiring better RAP skills is to communicate with others the results of the implementation of RAPs and to discuss methodology with others.

Students in graduate and undergraduate courses and participants in special training sessions can practice by doing a Mini-RAP. The Mini-RAP should be clearly defined as an educational activity and no more like a regular RAP than a five-minute practice interview is like a regular interview. A Mini-RAP requires a team of two or three people and a minimum of two cycles of data collection and analysis. There is usually no insider on a Mini-RAP team. The same requirements for informed consent apply. Students should be expected to present in class their interview transcripts, logs with coding, data-analysis diagramming, and "conclusions."

A Mini-RAP is a training activity and *not* a research activity.

There are three different training/orientation needs in the field. Individuals who will not be on the RAP team, but who may be providing support for the team or using the results of the team's work, will need an orientation on the process. Handouts for this type of orientation might include most of chapter 1. If possible, I would provide all members of the RAP team, including the insider on the team, with a copy of this book in advance of the orientation. A training of RAP trainers would probably require a minimum of two weeks, would be based on the book, and would include doing a regular RAP of at least four days.

Information on other resources for training are available on-line at the RAP-Research home page, <http://www.gonzaga.edu/RAP>.

APPENDIX D. GLOSSARY OF TERMS

Appreciative Inquiry – Inquiry that focuses on identifying what is going well in a situation, determining the conditions that make excellence possible, and encouraging those conditions within the organizational culture (Hammond and Hall 1998).

Bogus empowerment – Letting people think they have control over outcomes and the power to act on their own judgments when they actually do not have this control or power. This may involve giving responsibility without control. It can be the unintended consequence of hyperbole about the democratic nature of an organization (Ciulla 1998).

Coding – Part of the data analysis process consisting of the application of a limited number of labels to thought units (sentences, paragraphs, several paragraphs, or even individual words). Coding can be thought of as cutting the log of an interview into strips and placing the strips into piles. The labels for the piles are codes. Codes are based on threads that tie together bits of data. One usually starts with only five or six major codes and, if necessary, divides these codes into subcodes. Not all thought units are coded and some thought units can have multiple codes.

Culture – Traditionally used by social scientists to describe nearly everything that has been learned or produced by a group of people. A more limited definition restricts the concept to the knowledge people gather, share, and use to generate and interpret social behavior (Spradley and McCurdy 1972).

Data collection – The systematic gathering of facts, figures, and information from which conclusions can be inferred. For RAP, this includes information collected in advance, what is observed, and what is heard.

Semistructured interviews are a significant data-collection technique for RAP.

Data display – Part of the data analysis process for exploring the relationship between different pieces of information in which the goal is drawing conclusions. Data is usually displayed in the form of tables, charts, graphs, or drawings (Miles and Huberman 1994).

Emic understanding – Understanding based on the categories the local people use for dividing up their reality and identifying the terms they use for these categories (Pelto and Pelto 1978).

Etic understanding – Understanding based on the categories used by the researchers or outsiders to divide up reality.

Ethnography – A descriptive study of an intact cultural or social group or an individual or individuals within the group based primarily on participant observation and open-ended interviews. Reference to cultural terms helps differentiate ethnography from other qualitative research methods (Wolcott 1987). Ethnography is based on learning from people as opposed to studying people (Spradley and McCurdy 1972).

Field notes – The usually handwritten notes that are done as the data is being collected (Ely et al. 1991). Transcripts of interviews that were recorded can be called field notes or transcripts.

Fieldwork – The process of interacting and gathering information at the site or sites where a culture-sharing group is studied. The goal is to develop a portrait of a culture-sharing group. The assumption is that the researcher will spend a prolonged period at the site (Creswell 1998).

Individual respondents – Individuals who are interviewed about their own experience and not about knowledge of the broader system beyond their own experience. Individuals should be selected to represent variability. It should be clear to both the respondent and team members asking the questions that the questions concern only the individual's knowledge and behavior, and not what he or she thinks about the knowledge and behavior of others (see **Participants**).

Informed consent – Permission provided by the participants in a study for the researcher to use the information participants provide. Permission should be based upon an understanding of the activity and the uses that will be made of the results. It should indicate that participation is voluntary and that the individual knows that he or she can withdraw at any time.

Insiders –Team members or participants in social science research who are identified by the social group being studied as members in good standing. Traditional social science research has focused on efforts by investigators who have traditionally been outsiders trying to understand what the insiders believe, value, practice, and expect. There is a growing realization that insiders should play a role in the design, implementation, and publication of research (Van Maanen et al. 1996).

Iterative process – A process in which replications of a cycle produce results that approximate the desired result more and more closely. For RAP, the process describes the cycle of data analysis and data collection designed to produce better and better results. This same approach is labeled by some social scientists as a recursive process.

Key informants – Persons interviewed about the broader system and selected because of their experience and knowledge. It should be clear to the team members asking the questions and to the respondent that the questions concern what the respondent thinks about the knowledge and behavior of others (see **Participants**).

Local community – The individuals in a culture-sharing group who are the subject of the RAP. Members of a local community do not need to be in one physical location. Members of a local community are sometimes identified as "local people" (See **Insiders**).

Log – Logs are written documents that are the repositories of information from the field notes and transcripts, recorded in a format ready for analysis. Logs are a chronological record of what the team learns and its insights, and will include MEMOS. They are usually most useful if typed and double-spaced, with very large margins on both sides. Lines may be numbered. They are usually prepared at a location away from where the observations were collected. Field notes and memory can be used to fill in missing words from transcripts to make logs more accurate.

Margin remarks – Remarks written into the right-hand margin of the log after it has been typed. Almost anything can be included in a margin remark, but often these remarks are related to the coding activity. Some margin remarks suggest new interpretations and connections with other parts of the data and identify themes involving several different codes.

Member checking – Before the conclusions are final, the RAP team's sharing of the conclusions with the people who have provided the information, to check with them as to whether they agree with the analysis by the team. This can be done either formally or informally, but it should be made clear that the local people are expected to provide corrections to facts and to suggest their interpretation.

MEMOS – Reflections of the researcher, often notes to oneself about what has occurred, what has been learned, insights, and leads for future action (Ely et al. 1991, 80). Also called "observer comments", "analytic memos," or "researcher memos." It is recommended that in a RAP log, MEMO be spelled with all uppercase letters and that their contents be included in square brackets "[ ]" to remind the team of the importance of not confusing reflections with observations (things heard or observed). Memos should be dated and, for a RAP, their author should be identified.

Metaphor – A figure of speech in which a word or phrase, literally denoting one kind of object or idea, is used in place of another to suggest a likeness or analogy between them.

PRA (see **Participatory appraisal**).

Participants – Persons interviewed as part of the RAP process. "Participants" can be used interchangeably with "informants" or "respondents" when these terms are not modified with the words "individual" or "key." The term "subjects" is generally avoided.

Participant observation – A qualitative inquiry technique that requires more than simply being there and passively watching. This technique requires intensive observing, listening, and speaking to systematically explore relationships among different events while recording what is seen and heard (Ely et al. 1991).

Participatory appraisal – A rapid/relaxed approach to research designed to enable local people to share, embrace, and analyze their knowledge of life and to plan and act based on mapping, diagramming, and comparison. The assumption is that local people will do almost all of the investigation and analysis and will then share with the outsiders (Chambers and Blackburn 1996).

Propriety – Using procedures that are ethical, and fair to those involved and affected by the results of the assessment.

Qualitative research/qualitative inquiry – Attempts to understand experience as the participants feel it and to interpret phenomena in terms of the meaning people bring to them. Studies are conducted in their natural settings (Denzin and Lincoln 1994). The researcher is an instrument of data collection and is required to suspend preconceptions about the topics under investigation (Miles and Huberman 1994). Qualitative research is based on a few cases and many variables, whereas quantitative research works with a few variables and many cases (Ragin 1987 as cited in Creswell 1998).

Questionnaire research/survey research – Research based on questionnaires, a group of written questions to which individuals respond. Questionnaires are often administered to a sample of subjects drawn from a population (a survey) where the objective is to be able to make inferences about the population. Even though questionnaire research and survey research are distinct methodologies, the terms are used interchangeably in this book to identify research in which specific questions are prepared in advance based on the assumption that local categories and words are known and that enough is known of the local situation to identify important issues.

RAP (see **Rapid Assessment Process**).

Rapid Appraisal, Rapid Assessment, Rapid Rural Appraisal – Despite differences in details, there is general consensus that these terms describe research based on small multidisciplinary teams using semistructured interviews and direct observations to collect information, and that the entire process can be completed in one to six weeks.

Rapid Assessment Process (RAP) – Intensive, team-based qualitative inquiry using triangulation, iterative data analysis, and additional data collection to quickly develop a preliminary understanding of a situation from the insider's perspective.

Rapid research methods – Approaches to research designed to address the need for cost-effective and timely results in rapidly changing situations. These methods share some of the characteristics of qualitative or ethnographic research. The objective for most of these approaches can be summarized as first-cut assessments of poorly known areas (Conservation International 1991, 1). An element of compromise is recognized when rapid research methods are described as being "fairly quick and fairly clean." (Chambers 1991, 521).

Reliability – The consistency of a measure from one use to the next. When repeated measurements of the same thing give similar results, the measurement is said to be reliable.

Research tourism – An investigation that involves a quick visit to a study area and contact with the most easily reached local participants.

Rich picture – A drawing to which all the participants in an activity are encouraged to contribute. The use of rich pictures assumes that drawing diagrams and pictures allows individuals to express and check information in ways that can be more valid than talk and that, often, pictures are a better means for recording relationships and connections. Rich pictures are an element of Soft Systems Methodology (Checkland and Scholes 1990, 45).

Semistructured interview – An interview using open-ended questions or probes designed to get local people to talk about a subject and not just answer specific questions. Also, a dialogue or process in which important information develops out of directed conversation. Guidelines for semistructured interviews should be viewed as a memory aid and not as an agenda to be diligently worked through. This method contrasts with the structured interview, in which identical questions are asked of every informant.

Social science voyeurism – The practice by some social science researchers of observing or making inquiries on human behavior and practices to satisfy or gratify their own curiosity. Usually implies collecting more information than is necessary.

Soft Systems Methodology – An approach for rigorously considering messy and value-laden situations based on steps that include (1) identifying a situation which has provoked concern, (2) selecting some relevant human activity system and making a model of the activity, (3) using the model to question the real-world situation, and (4) using the debate initiated by the comparison to define action which would improve the original problem situation. Developing a rich picture is a critical element of Soft Systems Methodology (Checkland and Scholes 1990).

Sondeo – Term used by the Guatemalan Institute of Agricultural Science and Technology to describe a modified survey technique for understanding the cropping or farming systems of farmers. Based on the use of multidisciplinary teams, semistructured interviews with farmers, and direct observation over a six- to ten-day period (Hildebrand 1981).

Tag-team interviewing – An unintended perception of the group interview process by respondents who feel like they are being attacked by a gang of inquisitors trying to beat answers out of an uncooperative witness. A focus on getting respondents to tell their stories, as opposed to answering the questions of the researcher, and a relaxed, conversational tone can prevent the perception of tag-team interviewing.

Triangulation – A term from navigation and physical surveying that describes an operation for determining a position by using bearings from two known fixed points so that the three points form a triangle. Triangulation is used as a metaphor by social scientists for the use of data from different sources, the use of several different researchers, the use of multiple perspectives to interpret a single set of data, and the use of multiple methods to study a single problem.

Validity – A term to describe an instrument measuring what it is supposed to measure. Even when measurements are reliable, consistent from one use to the next, they can be invalid. Some qualitative researchers propose the use of the term "trustworthiness" instead of "validity" and "reliability" (Ely et al. 1991).

REFERENCES

Abalu, G. O. I., N. M. Fisher, and Y. Abdullahi.
1987. Rapid rural appraisal for generating appropriate technologies for peasant farmers: Some experiences from northern Nigeria. *Agricultural Systems* 25: 311–24.

Abate, T.
1992. Environmental rapid-assessment programs have appeal and critics. *BioScience* 42: 486–89.

Aigbe, S. A.
1996. Garage anthropology: Using symbiotic indicators as a rapid appraisal technique in social work. *High Plains Applied Anthropologist* 16(1): 86–91.

Anker, M.
1991. Epidemiological and statistical methods for rapid health assessment: Introduction. *World Health Statistical Quarterly* 44(3).

Anker, M., S. Guidotti, S. Orzeszyna, S. A. Sapirie, and M. C. Thuriaux.
1993. Rapid evaluation methods (REM) of health services performance: Methodological observations. *Bulletin of the World Health Organization* 71(1): 15–21.

Astone, J.
1998. Incorporating local history into planning documents: A case study from Guinea, West Africa. *World Development* 26: 1773–84.

Bartunek, J. M., and M. R. Louis.
1996. *Insider/outsider research.* Thousand Oaks, Calif.: Sage.

Becker, H. S.
1986. *Writing for social scientists.* Chicago: University of Chicago Press.

REFERENCES

Beebe, J.
1982. *Rapid rural appraisal, Umm Hijliij Breimya, El Obeid, Northern Kordolan.* Khartoum, Sudan: U.S. Agency for International Development.

1994. Concept of the average farmer and putting the farmer first. *Journal of Farming Systems Research-Extension* 4(3): 1–16.

1995. Basic concepts and techniques of rapid appraisal. *Human Organization* 54(1): 42–51.

Bernard, H. R.
1995. *Research methods in anthropology: Qualitative and quantitative approaches.* 2d ed. Walnut Creek, Calif.: AltaMira.

Bogdan, R., and S. K. Biklen.
1992. *Qualitative research for education: An introduction to theory and methods.* 2d ed. Boston: Allyn & Bacon.

Booth, W.
1979. *Critical understanding: The powers and limits of pluralism.* Chicago: University of Chicago Press.

Bostain, J. C.
1970. *Suggestions for efficient use of an untrained interpreter.* Washington, D.C.: U.S. Department of State.

Bottrall, A.
1981. *Comparative study of the management and organization of irrigation projects.* World Bank Staff Working Paper no. 458. Washington, D.C.: World Bank.

Bradfield, S.
1981. Appropriate methodology for appropriate technology. In *Transferring technology for small-scale farmers*, 23–33. American Society for Agronomy.

BRIDGES (Briefings in Development and Gender).
1994. *Annotated bibliography on gender, rapid rural appraisal and participatory rural appraisal.* Brighton, England: Institute of Development Studies, University of Sussex.

Brush, S. B.
1986. Basic and applied-research in farming systems: An anthropologist's appraisal. *Human Organization* 45(3): 220–28.

Burgess, R.
1982. The unstructured interview as a conversation. In *Field research: A source-book and field manual*, ed. R. Burgess, 107–10. London: Allen and Unwin.

Campa, A., and B. Skartvedt.
1997. Rapid appraisal of four Denver neighborhoods: A pilot study of community strengths and weaknesses. *High Plains Applied Anthropologist* 17(2): 131–44.

Carruthers, I., and R. Chambers.
1981. Rapid appraisal for rural development. *Agricultural Administration* 8: 407–22.

CASL (Community Adaptation and Sustainable Livelihoods).
1999. *Participatory research for sustainable livelihoods: A guide for field projects on adaptive strategies: Participatory Rural Appraisal (PRA)*. Retrieved July 6, 2000, from <http://iisd1.iisd.ca/casl/CASLGuide/PRA.htm>.

Chambers, R.
1979. Rural development tourism: Poverty unperceived. Paper presented at the Rapid Rural Appraisal Conference at the Institute of Development Studies, University of Sussex, Brighton, England.

1980. Shortcut methods in information gathering for rural development projects. Paper presented at the World Bank Agricultural Sector Symposium, Institute of Development Studies, University of Sussex, Brighton, England.

1983. Rapid appraisal for improving existing canal irrigation systems. Discussion Paper Series. New Delhi, India: Ford Foundation.

1991. Shortcut and participatory methods for gaining social information for projects. In *Putting people first: Sociological variables in rural development*, ed. M. M. Cernea, 515–37. 2d ed. Washington, D.C.: Oxford University Press, World Bank.

1996. *Introduction to participatory approaches and methodologies*. Retrieved June 15, 1999, from <http://www.ids.ac.uk/ids/particip/intro/introind.html>.

1999. Relaxed and participatory appraisal: Notes on practical approaches and methods. Presentation at the PRA Familiarisation Workshop, Institute of Development Studies, University of Sussex, Brighton, England.

REFERENCES

Chambers, R., and J. Blackburn.
1996. The power of participation. IDS Policy Briefing Issue. Brighton, England: Institute of Development Studies, University of Sussex.

Checkland, P., and J. Scholes.
1990. *Soft systems methodology in action*. Chichester, England: John Wiley & Sons.

Ciulla, J. B.
1998. Leadership and the problem of bogus empowerment. In *Ethics: The heart of leadership*, ed. J. B. Ciulla, 63–86. Westport, Conn.: Quorum Books.

Clark University Program for International Development and Kenya Ministry of Environment and Natural Resources, National Environment Secretariat (CUNES).
1989. *An introduction to participatory rural appraisal for rural resources management*. Worcester, Mass.: Program for International Development, Clark University.

Clement, U.
1990. Surveys of heterosexual behaviour. *Annual Review of Sex Research* 1: 45–74.

Collinson, M.
1979. Rapid rural appraisal: Understanding small farmers. Paper presented at the Rapid Rural Appraisal Conference at the Institute of Development Studies, University of Sussex, Brighton, England.

1981. A low cost approach to understanding small farmers. *Agricultural Administration* 8: 463–71.

Conservation International.
1991. *A biological assessment of the Alto Madidi Region and adjacent areas of Northwest Bolivia*. Rapid Assessment Program, RAP Working Papers no. 1. Washington, D.C.: Conservation International.

Creswell, J. W.
1998. *Qualitative inquiry and research design: Choosing among five traditions*. Thousand Oaks, Calif.: Sage.

Dale, J., and C. Shipman.
1996. Creating a shared vision of out of hours care: Using rapid appraisal methods to create an interagency, community oriented, approach to service development. *British Medical Journal* 312: 1206–10.

Denzin, N. K., and Y. S. Lincoln.
1994. *Handbook of qualitative research.* Thousand Oaks, Calif.: Sage.

Dole, D., and D. Cooperrider.
2000. *The appreciative inquiry resource list.* Retrieved August 15, 2000, from <http://www.serve.com/taos/appreciative.html>.

Doorman, F.
1990. A social-science contribution to applied agricultural-research for the small farm sector: The diagnostic case-study as a tool for problem identification. *Agricultural Systems* 32(3): 273–90.

Dunn, T.
1994. Rapid rural appraisal: A description of the methodology and its application in teaching and research at Charles Stuart University. *Rural Society* 4(3/4): 2–7.

Ely, M., M. Anzul, T. Friedman, D. Garner, and A. M. Steinmetz.
1991. *Doing qualitative research: Circles within circles.* Bristol, Pa.: Falmer Press.

Epstein, S. T.
1992. The relationship between rapid rural appraisal (RRA) and development market research (DMR). In *RAP: Rapid assessment procedures. Qualitative methodologies for planning and evaluation of health related programmes,* ed. N. S. Schrimshaw and G. R. Gleason, 365–75. Boston: International Nutrition Foundation for Developing Countries.

Erickson, K., and D. Stull.
1998. *Doing team ethnography: Warnings and advice.* Thousand Oaks, Calif.: Sage.

Ervin, A. M.
1997. Trying the impossible: Relatively "rapid" methods in a city-wide needs assessment. *Human Organization* 56(4): 379–87.

Fetterman, D. M.
1989. *Ethnography: Step by step.* Newbury Park, Calif.: Sage.

1998. *Ethnography: Step by step.* 2d ed. Thousand Oaks, Calif.: Sage.

2000. *Ethnography and the Internet.* Retrieved August 15, 2000, from <http://www.stanford.edu/~davidf/ethnography.html>.

Fielding, N. G., and J. L. Fielding.
1986. *Linking data.* Beverly Hills, Calif.: Sage.

Flick, U.
1992. Triangulation revisited: Strategy of validation. *Journal for the Theory of Social Behavior* 22(2): 175–97.

Fluehr-Lobban, C.
1998. Ethics. In *Handbook of methods in cultural anthropology,* ed. H. R. Bernard. Walnut Creek, Calif.: AltaMira.

Galt, D.
1987. How rapid rural appraisal and other socio-economic diagnostic techniques fit into the cyclic FSR/E process. In *Proceedings of the 1985 International Conference on Rapid Rural Appraisal,* Khon Kaen University, 207–27. Khon Kaen, Thailand: Rural Systems Research and Farming Systems Research Projects.

Ginsburg, R. N., P. Kramer, J. Lang, P. Sale, and R. Steneck.
1998. *Revised rapid assessment protocol (RAP).* Retrieved June 6, 1999, from <http://coral.aoml.noaa.gov/agra/rap-revised.html>.

Giorgi, A.
1989. One type of analysis of descriptive data: Procedures involved in following a scientific phenomenological method. *Journal of Human Science:* 39–61.

Gittelsohn, J., P. Pelto, M. Bentley, K. Bhattacharyya, and J. Jensen.
1998. *Rapid Assessment Procedures (RAP): Ethnographic methods to investigate women's health.* Boston: International Nutrition Foundation.

Goetz, J. P., and M. D. LeCompte.
1984. *Ethnography and qualitative design in educational research.* New York: Academic Press.

Gow, D. D.
1991. Collaboration in development consulting: Stooges, hired guns, or musketeers? *Human Organization* 50(1): 1–15.

Grandstaff, T. B., and S. W. Grandstaff.
1987. A conceptual basis for methodological development in rapid rural appraisal. In *Proceedings of the 1985 International Conference on Rapid Rural Ap-*

praisal, Khon Kaen University, 69–88. Khon Kaen, Thailand: Rural Systems Research and Farming Systems Research Projects.

Guyton, W.
1992. *Guidelines for marketing information needs assessments (MINAs): AMIS project.* Quezon City, Philippines: Abt Associates.

Hammersley, M., and P. Atkinson.
1995. *Ethnography: Principles in practice.* 2d ed. New York: Routledge.

Hammond, S. A.
1998. *The thin book of appreciative inquiry.* 2d ed. Plano, Tex.: Thin Books.

Hammond, S. A, and J. Hall.
1998. *Thin Book Publishing Co.: What is appreciative inquiry?* Retrieved July 6, 1999, from <http://www.thinbook.com/thinbook/chap1fromle.html>.

Handwerker, W. P.
2001. *Quick ethnography: A guide to rapid multi-method research.* Walnut Creek, Calif.: AltaMira.

Harris, K. J., N. W. Jerome, and S. B. Fawcett.
1997. Rapid assessment procedures: A review and critique. *Human Organization* 56(3): 375–78.

Hassin-Brack, J.
1988. *Rapid rural appraisal: Annotated bibliography.* Tucson, Ariz.: University of Arizona, Arid Land Center, for the U. S. Department of Agriculture.

Heifetz, R. D.
1994. *Leadership without easy answers.* Cambridge, Mass.: Belknap.

Henderson, L.
1995. *Epidemiologic trends in drug abuse, advance report.* Retrieved January 12, 2000, from <http://www.cdmgroup.com/cewg/docs/695–Chic/Docs/sum95adv.html>.

Herman, E. and M. Bentley.
1993. *Rapid Assessment Procedures (RAP) to improve the household management of diarrhea.* Boston: International Foundation for Developing Countries.

Hildebrand, P. E.
1979. Summary of the Sondeo methodology used by ICTA. Paper presented at the Rapid Rural Appraisal Conference at the Institute of Development Studies, University of Sussex, Brighton, England.

REFERENCES

1981. Combining disciplines in rapid appraisal: The Sondea approach. *Agricultural Administration* 8: 423–32.

1982. Summary of the Sondeo methodology used by ICTA. In *Farming systems research and development: Guidelines for developing countries*, ed. W. W. Shaner, P. F. Philipp, and W. R. Schmehl, 289–91. Boulder, Colo.: Westview.

Honadle, G.
1979. Rapid reconnaissance approaches to organizational analysis for development administration. Organization and Administration of Integrated Rural Development, Working Paper no. 1. Washington, D.C.: Development Alternatives.

1982. Rapid reconnaissance for development administration: Mapping and moulding organizational landscapes. *World Development* 10(8): 633–49.

Huberman, A. M., and M. B. Miles.
1994. Data management and analysis methods. In *Handbook of qualitative research*, ed. M. K. Denzin and Y. S. Lincoln, 428–44. Thousand Oaks, Calif.: Sage.

Institute of Development Studies.
1996. *The power of participation*. IDS Policy Briefing no. 7.

Janesick, V.
1994. The dance of qualitative research design: Metaphor, methodolatry, and meaning. In *Handbook of Qualitative Research*, ed. N. K. Denzin and Y. S. Lincoln, 209–19. Thousand Oaks, Calif.: Sage.

Khon Kaen University.
1987. *Proceedings of the 1985 International Conference on Rapid Rural Appraisal*. Khon Kaen, Thailand: Rural Systems Research and Farming Systems Research Projects.

Kumar, K.
1987. *Conducting group interviews in developing countries*. AID Program Design and Evaluation Methodology Report no. 8. Washington, D.C.: U.S. Agency for International Development.

1993. *Rapid appraisal methods*. Washington, D.C.: World Bank.

la Gra, J.

1990. *A commodity system assessment methodology for problem and project identification.* Moscow: University of Idaho, College of Agriculture, Postharvest Institute for Perishables.

Lagacé, R. O.

1970. The HRAF data quality control schedule. *Behavior Science Notes* 5(2): 125–32.

Lee, R. M.

1994. *Dangerous fieldwork.* Thousands Oaks, Calif.: Sage.

Leurs, R.

1997. Critical reflections on rapid and participatory rural appraisal. *Development in Practice* 7(3): 291–93.

Lincoln, Y. S., and E. G. Guba.

1985. *Naturalistic inquiry.* Beverly Hills, Calif.: Sage.

Lofland, J., and L. H. Lofland.

1984. *Analyzing social settings: A guide to qualitative observation and analysis.* 2d ed. Belmont, Calif.: Wadsworth.

Macintyre, K.

1995. The case for rapid assessment surveys for family planning program evaluation. Paper presented at the Annual Meeting of the Population Association of America, University of North Carolina at Chapel Hill.

Manderson, L.

1998. Applying medical anthropology in the control of infectious disease. *Tropical Medicine & International Health* 3(12): 1020–27.

Market Navigation.

2000. *How to get beneath the surface in focus groups.* Retrieved July 2, 2000, from <http://www.mnav.com/bensurf.html>.

Marshall, C., and G. B. Rossman.

1999. *Designing qualitative research.* 3d ed. Thousand Oaks, Calif.: Sage.

Mathison, S.

1988. Why triangulate? *Educational Researcher* 17(2): 13–17.

Matzke, G.

1995. A rapid appraisal method for approximating wildlife presence and relative abundance. *African Journal of Ecology* 33: 266–70.

REFERENCES

McCracken, J. A.
1988. A working framework for rapid rural appraisal: Lessons from a Fiji experience. *Agricultural Administration and Extension* 29(3): 163–84.

Menegay, M., C. Milona, R. Millendez, R. Quero, and R. Alberto.
1990. *User's manual on the fundamental analytics for rapid marketing appraisals in the Philippines.* Quezon City, Philippines: Department of Agriculture.

Metzler, K.
1997. *Creative interviewing: The writer's guide to gathering information by asking questions.* 3d ed. New York: Allyn & Bacon.

Miles, M. B., and A. M. Huberman.
1984. *Qualitative data analysis: A sourcebook of new methods.* Beverly Hills, Calif.: Sage.

1994. *Qualitative data analysis: An expanded sourcebook.* 2d ed. Thousand Oaks, Calif.: Sage.

Mirvis, P. H., and S. E. Seashore.
1982. Creating ethical relationships in organizational research. In *The ethics of social research,* vol. 1, *Surveys and experiments,* ed. J. E. Sieber, 79–104. New York: Springer-Verlag.

Morgan, D. L.
1997. *Focus groups as qualitative research.* 2d ed. Thousand Oaks, Calif.: Sage.

Murray, S. A.
1999. Experiences with "rapid appraisal" in primary care: Involving the public in assessing health needs, orienting staff, and educating medical students. *British Medical Journal* 318: 440–44.

NOAA's Damage Assessment and Restoration Staff.
1997. *Rapid Assessment Program.* Retrieved July 6, 2000, from <http://www.darp.noaa.gov/darporg/rap.html>.

Overseas Development Administration.
1995. *Guidance note on how to do stakeholder analysis of AID projects and programmes.* Retrieved June 30, 2000, from <http://carryon.oneworld.org/uforic/gb/stake1.html>.

Patton, M. Q.
1990. *Qualitative evaluation and research methods.* 2d ed. Newbury Park, Calif.: Sage.

Pelto, P. J., and G. H. Pelto.
1978. *Anthropological research: The structure of inquiry.* Cambridge: Cambridge University Press.

Phillips, R. S.
1993. Geographic knowledge and survey research. *International Journal of Public Opinion Research* 5(1): 100–104.

Pido, M. D.
1995. The application of rapid rural appraisal techniques in coastal resources planning: Experience in Malampaya Sound, Philippines. *Ocean and Coastal Management* 26(1): 57–72.

Ragin, C. C.
1987. *The comparative method: Moving beyond qualitative and quantitative strategies.* Berkeley: University of California Press.

Ratner, M. S.
1996. Many routes to homeownership: A four-site ethnographic study of minority and immigrant experiences. *Housing Policy Debate* 7(1): 103–45.

Reeves, E. B., and T. Frankenberger.
1981. *Socio-economic constraints to the production, distribution, and consumption of millet, sorghum, and cash crops in North Kordofan, Sudan.* Lexington: University of Kentucky.

Rhoades, R. E.
1982. *The art of the informal agricultural survey.* Lima, Peru: International Potato Center.

1987. Basic field techniques for Rapid Rural Appraisal. In *Proceedings of the 1985 International Conference on Rapid Rural Appraisal,* Khon Kaen University, 114–28. Khon Kaen, Thailand: Rural Systems Research and Farming Systems Research Projects.

Rhodes, T., and G. V. Stimson.
1998. *The rapid assessment and response guide on substance use and sexual risk behaviour (SEX-RAR).* Geneva, Switzerland: World Health Organization, Programme on Substance Use.

Richardson, L.
1994. Writing: A method of inquiry. In *Handbook of qualitative research,* ed. N. K. Denzin and Y. S. Lincoln, 516–29. Thousands Oaks, Calif.: Sage.

REFERENCES

Rifkin, S. B.

1996. Rapid rural appraisal: Its use and value for health planners and managers. *Public Administration* 74(Autumn): 509–26.

Robb, C. M.

1999. *Can the poor influence policy? Participatory poverty assessments in the developing world.* Washington, D.C.: World Bank.

Salamon, S., R. L. Farnsworth, and J. A. Rendziak.

1998. Is locally led conservation planning working? A farm town case study. *Rural Sociology* 63(2): 214–34.

Schensul, J. J., and M. D. LeCompte.

1999. *Ethonographer's toolkit.* 7 vols. Walnut Creek, Calif.: AltaMira.

Scrimshaw, N., and G. R. Gleason.

1992. *Rapid assessment procedures: Qualitative methodologies for planning and evaluation of health related programmes.* Boston: International Nutrition Foundation for Developing Countries.

Scrimshaw, S. C. M.

1992. Adaptation of anthropological methodologies to rapid assessment of nutrition and primary health care. In *RAP: Rapid assessment procedures. Qualitative methodologies for planning and evaluation of health related programmes,* ed. N. S. Scrimshaw and G. R. Gleason, 24–37. Boston: International Nutrition Foundation for Developing Countries.

Shaner, W. W., P. F. Philipp, and W. R. Schmehl.

1982. *Farming systems research and development: Guidelines for developing countries.* Boulder, Colo.: Westview.

Sherman, R. R., and R. B. Webb.

1988. *Qualitative research in education: Focus and method.* New York: Falmer Press.

Smith, R., comp.

1999. *Annotated bibliography: Readings in research methods in community economic development.* Retrieved July 30, 2000, from <http://virtual-u.ssfu. ca/cedc/forestcomm/pprworking/ABsmith.htm>.

South Florida Water Management District.

1997. *Wetland Rapid Assessment Program.* Retrieved July 6, 2000, from <http://www.sfwmd.gov/org/reg/wrap99.htm>.

Spradley, J. P.
1979. *The ethnographic interview.* New York: Holt, Reinhart and Winston.

1980. *Participant observation.* New York: Holt, Reinhart and Winston.

Spradley, J. P., and D. W. McCurdy.
1972. *The cultural experience: Ethnography in complex society.* Kingsport, Tenn.: Science Research Associates.

Stone, L., and J. G. Campbell.
1984. The use and misuse of surveys in international development: An experiment from Nepal. *Human Organization* 43(1): 27–37.

Strauss, A., and J. Corbin.
1990. *Basics of qualitative research: Grounded theory procedures and techniques.* Thousand Oaks, Calif.: Sage.

Sturges, P., and G. Chimseu.
1996. The chain of information provision in the villages of Malawi: A rapid rural appraisal. *International Information and Library Review* 28: 135–56.

Tesch, R.
1990. *Qualitative research: Analysis and types of software tools.* New York: Falmer Press.

Thompson, L.
1970. Exploring American Indian communities in depth. In *Women in the field: Anthropological experiences,* ed. P. Golde, 45–64. Chicago: Aldine.

Townsley, P.
1996. *Rapid rural appraisal, participatory rural appraisal and aquaculture.* FAO Fisheries Technical Paper no. 358. Rome: Food and Agriculture Organization.

Umans, L.
1997. The rapid appraisal of a knowledge system: The health system of Guarani Indians in Bolivia. *Indigenous Knowledge and Development Monitor* 5(3): 11–14.

UNFPA (United Nations Population Fund).
1997. *Population and reproductive health programmes: Applying rapid anthropological assessment procedures.* New York: Technical and Evaluation Division, UNFPA.

REFERENCES

USAID (United States Agency for International Development).
2000. *Internet guide for participation.* Retrieved July 30, 2000, from <http://www.usaid.gov/about/part_devel/docs/webguide.htm>.

Van der Stichele, P.
1998. *A new approach for research and the design of communication for development strategies and programmes.* Retrieved June 17, 1999, from<http://www.fao.org/sd/CDdirect/CDan0015.htm>.

Van Horn, L. F., A. R. Hagood, and G. J. Sorensen.
1996. Wounded Knee, 1890 and today: A special resource study for planning alternatives. *Landscape and Urban Planning* 36: 135–58.

Van Maanen, J., P. K. Manning, and M. L. Miller.
1996. Series editors' introduction. In *Insider/outsider team research,* ed. J. M. Bartunek and M. R. Louis, v–vi. Thousand Oaks, Calif.: Sage.

1998. Series editors' introduction. In *Doing team ethnography: Warnings and advice,* ed. K. Erickson and D. Stull, vi–vii. Thousand Oaks, Calif.: Sage.

Van Willigen, J., and T. L. Finan.
1991. *Soundings: Rapid and reliable research methods for practicing anthropologists.* Washington, D.C.: American Anthropological Association.

Vlassoff, C., and M. Tanner.
1992. The relevance of rapid assessment to health research and interventions. *Health Policy and Planning* 7: 1–9.

Webb, S., and B. Webb.
1932. *Methods of social study.* London: Longmans, Green.

Werner, O., and D. T. Campbell.
1970. Translating, working through interpreters, and the problem of decentering. In *A handbook of method in cultural anthropology,* ed. R. Naroll and R. Cohen, 398–420. New York: Columbia University Press.

Williams, B., and T. Ramos.
1997. *Rapid ethnographic assessment: Park users and neighbors: Civil war defenses of Washington and Anacostia Park, District of Columbia, for park management plans.* Denver, Colo.: Denver Service Center, National Park Service.

Wilson, K. K., and G. Morren, Jr.
1990. *Systems approaches for improvement in agriculture and resource management.* New York: MacMillan.

REFERENCES

Wolcott, H. F.

1987. *On ethnographic intent*. Hillsdale, N.J.: Lawrence Erlbaum.

1994. *Transforming qualitative data*. Thousand Oaks, Calif.: Sage.

1995. *The art of fieldwork*. Walnut Creek, Calif.: AltaMira.

1999. Ethnography: A way of seeing. Walnut Creek, Calif.: AltaMira.

SUBJECT INDEX

AUTHOR INDEX

ABOUT THE AUTHOR

James Beebe is a professor in the Doctoral Program in Leadership Studies at Gonzaga University in Spokane, Washington. He identifies himself as a practitioner/scholar. His first experience with international development was as a Peace Corps volunteer in the Philippines. While there, he started graduate work in anthropology at the University of the Philippines. He completed a Ph.D. in international development education, an M.A. in anthropology, and an M.A. in food research (international agricultural development) at Stanford University. For his dissertation, he did a year of fieldwork in a village in the Philippines. He has taught at the Monterey Institute of International Studies and Oregon State University and has delivered lectures at numerous universities, including Cornell, Harvard, UCLA, the University of Florida, and the University of Pretoria. While working for the U.S. Agency for International Development, he had long-term assignments in Sudan, the Philippines, Liberia, and South Africa and short-term assignments in another nine countries. He has spent more that twenty years outside the United States. In addition to his interests in qualitative research methodology, he is also involved in research and does consulting on the relationship of leadership and technology.

8/02